Bangladeshi Literature in English

This pioneering book brings together several critical essays on Bangladeshi writers in the English language, both at home and abroad, and interviews with a prominent poet and a novelist.

The past years have seen various attempts to conceptualize and debate the tradition of Bangladeshi literature in English. English has been in Bengal, which included the geographical territory that constitutes present-day Bangladesh, since the arrival of Ralph Fitch in 1583, and although Bengalis started experimenting creatively in the language in the late eighteenth and early nineteenth centuries, the tradition suffered significant setbacks in Bangladesh and remained in a semi-muzzled state for various political and cultural reasons discussed in the book, before and after independence. However, the tradition has seen a surge since the 1990s, and several writers have emerged on home soil and in places where Bangladeshis have settled, including Australia, Canada, Sweden, the UK, and the USA. The book provides an overview of this tradition and investigates the various thematic and stylistic issues in the works of the selected writers, suggesting the vibrancy and versatility of this evolving national and postcolonial literary stream.

The book will be of interest to researchers, academics, and scholars in the field of Bangladeshi writing in English, Southeast Asian literature, Asian literature, diaspora, and literary studies. The chapters in this book were originally published in the *Journal of Postcolonial Writing.*

Mohammad A. Quayum is a full-time researcher and Professor in the College of Humanities, Arts and Social Sciences at Flinders University, Australia. He taught at universities in Bangladesh, Malaysia, Singapore, and the US before returning to his *alma mater*, Flinders University, in 2020. He is the author, editor, and translator of numerous books in the areas of American literature, Bengali literature, and Southeast Asian literature.

Md. Mahmudul Hasan is Professor of English and postcolonial literature at International Islamic University Malaysia. He completed a PhD in comparative literature at the University of Portsmouth, did a postdoctoral stint at the University of Heidelberg, and taught in the Department of English at the University of Dhaka. He has published in the fields of feminist, postcolonial, Islamic, South Asian, and Muslim diasporic literatures, as well as Islam and English studies.

Bangladeshi Literature in English

Critical Essays and Interviews

Edited by
Mohammad A. Quayum
and Md. Mahmudul Hasan

LONDON AND NEW YORK

First published 2024
by Routledge
4 Park Square, Milton Park, Abingdon, Oxon OX14 4RN

and by Routledge
605 Third Avenue, New York, NY 10158

Routledge is an imprint of the Taylor & Francis Group, an informa business

British Library Cataloguing in Publication Data
A catalogue record for this book is available from the British Library

ISBN13: 978-1-032-67035-5 (hbk)
ISBN13: 978-1-032-67036-2 (pbk)
ISBN13: 978-1-032-67039-3 (ebk)

DOI: 10.4324/9781032670393

Typeset in Minion Pro
by Newgen Publishing UK

Publisher's Note
The publisher accepts responsibility for any inconsistencies that may have arisen during the conversion of this book from journal articles to book chapters, namely the inclusion of journal terminology.

Contents

Citation Information

The following chapters were originally published in various volumes and issues of the *Journal of Postcolonial Writing*. When citing this material, please use the original page numbering for each article, as follows:

Chapter 1

Muslim Bengal writes back: A study of Rokeya's encounter with and representation of Europe
Md. Mahmudul Hasan
Journal of Postcolonial Writing, volume 52, issue 6 (2016), pp. 739–751

Chapter 2

Panchayat and colonialism in Humayun Kabir's Men and Rivers
Md. Mahmudul Hasan
Journal of Postcolonial Writing, volume 58, issue 6 (2022), pp. 744–757

Chapter 3

"Here I'll stay": Kaiser Haq's poems and the impact of being at home
Kathryn Hummel
Journal of Postcolonial Writing, volume 58, issue 6 (2022), pp. 758–772

Chapter 4

Toxic grace? Tahmima Anam's The Bones of Grace *and the pollution trade*
Md. Alamgir Hossain
Journal of Postcolonial Writing, volume 58, issue 6 (2022), pp. 773–786

Chapter 5

Beyond national(ist) binaries: The case of Zia Haider Rahman's In the Light of What We Know
Md Rezaul Haque
Journal of Postcolonial Writing, volume 58, issue 6 (2022), pp. 787–801

Chapter 6

Introducing a Bangladeshi writer in English: Interview with Kaiser Haq
Mohammad A. Quayum
Journal of Postcolonial Writing, volume 36, issue 1 (1997), pp. 110–119

Chapter 7

Delving beneath the surface: An interview with Monica Ali
Sadaf Saaz
Journal of Postcolonial Writing, volume 58, issue 6 (2022), pp. 802–816

Notes on Contributors

Md Rezaul Haque teaches in the English Department at St John's University, New York. He received his PhD from Flinders University, Australia, and completed an Endeavour Postdoctoral Research Fellowship in 2016. He has published internationally on Indian English fiction, Rokeya Sakhawat Hossain, Hasan Azizul Huq, and Bengali diasporic writers.

Md. Mahmudul Hasan is Professor of English and postcolonial literature at International Islamic University Malaysia. He completed a PhD in comparative literature at the University of Portsmouth, did a postdoctoral stint at the University of Heidelberg, and taught in the Department of English at the University of Dhaka. He has published in the fields of feminist, postcolonial, Islamic, South Asian, and Muslim diasporic literatures, as well as Islam and English studies.

Md. Alamgir Hossain is Associate Professor of English at the University of Rajshahi, Bangladesh. His research interests include postcolonial theory and literature, diaspora literature, world literature, critical ethnic studies, and the environmental humanities.

Kathryn Hummel is Associate Professor in the School of Law, Ajeenka DY Patil University, India. She holds a PhD in social sciences (communication and information studies) from the University of South Australia and her research focuses at the intersection of sociology, ethnography, cultural studies, and the arts.

Mohammad A. Quayum is a full-time researcher and Professor in the College of Humanities, Arts and Social Sciences at Flinders University, Australia. He taught at universities in Bangladesh, Malaysia, Singapore, and the US before returning to his *alma mater*, Flinders University, in 2020. He is the author, editor, and translator of numerous books in the areas of American literature, Bengali literature, and Southeast Asian literature.

Sadaf Saaz is a poet, writer, entrepreneur, molecular biologist, and women's rights advocate. She runs an arts production company Jatrik, and The Junction, a performance space, and has published the poetry collection *Sari Reams* (2013). Her monologues based on Bangladeshi women's stories, *Je Kotha Jai Na Bola* (That Which Cannot Be Said), have been performed in various locations in Bangladesh.

Introduction—Bangladeshi literature in English: A thrice-born tradition

Mohammad A. Quayum and Md. Mahmudul Hasan

The use of the phrase "thrice-born" in the title of this introduction has connotations of uneasy or interrupted beginnings. Perhaps we should start by clarifying that "thrice-born" here bears no relation to the Sanskrit word *dvija* or "twice-born" or the title of Meenakshi Mukherjee's (1971) book on Indian English novels, *The Twice Born Fiction. Dvija* is used in the Hindu social system to refer to the elitism and privilege of the three upper castes: Brahmins, Kshatriyas, and Vaishyas. Mukherjee uses the term "twice-born" to explain the derivative and hybrid nature of Indian English fiction, in which Indian tropes, thoughts, and dialogues are "translated" into the colonizer's speech. In contrast, we have used the expression "thrice-born" to suggest the evolutionary nature of Bangladeshi anglophone literature: that it has developed through three historical phases, during which the geographical territory that now constitutes Bangladesh has gone through several political rebirths and renamings: Bengal/East Bengal (1905–11),[1] East Pakistan (1947–71), and Bangladesh (1971–). To put it differently, although Bangladesh is a relatively new country, to gain a holistic picture of how the anglophone literary tradition has developed in this geographical space, one needs to look back to its beginnings during the British colonial period, take stock of English writings during the Pakistani phase, and, finally, investigate the state of the tradition and its challenges and achievements, especially after the country's attainment of self-rule in 1971. This will help establish the nature of cultural continuity in a land that has gone through a political whirlwind since the colonial era and been subjected to changes of political identity on multiple occasions.

English writing in British colonial (East) Bengal

English, as we know, is an imported tongue brought to the subcontinent by English people in the late 16th century. The first Englishman to set foot in India was the Jesuit Father Thomas Stephens (1549–1619), who arrived in 1578 to escape "religious persecution in Elizabethan England" (Dharwadker 2003, 202). However, the first Englishman to travel through Bengal, especially East Bengal (present-day Bangladesh), and write about his experiences was Ralph Fitch (1550–1611), who came to India in 1583 as one of a team of four people aiming to secure trading concessions from the Mughal Emperor Jalaluddin Akbar (Dharwadker 2003, 203–204).

From there on, the language continued to expand and spread, slowly but steadily, as more and more English traders arrived in that part of the world, mainly to work for the East India Company, founded in 1600. The situation changed radically in 1660 when Charles II empowered the East India Company to run its affairs in the subcontinent like a "virtual state" (Dharwadker 2003, 207). Two other historical events that further consolidated the position of the English language and helped its dispersion through the local communities were Robert Clive's victory over the then Nawab of Bengal, Siraj-ud-daula, at the Battle of Plassey in 1757, and the introduction of the English Education Act of 1835. These events effectively ensured the future of English, to quote Salman Rushdie (1997), as "a naturalised sub-continental language", much like Urdu before it (xi). By the end of the 19th century, Indians, and Bengalis in particular, who had been exposed for over two centuries to the language and its associated culture through employment, interracial marriages, personal friendships, and religious conversion by missionaries were adequately confident and competent to transmit their imagination in this transplanted medium.

The first Indian to use English as a mode of creative expression was Din Muhammad, or Sake Dean Mahomed (1759–1851), a Bengali Muslim from the Patna region of Odisha, then part of British Bengal. He published his travelogue, *The Travels of Dean Mahomet*, in 1794 in Cork, Ireland, encouraged by his Irish wife, Jane Daly. This marked the beginning of a counter-discourse on India, contesting its British representations inaugurated by Fitch's travel account that first appeared in Richard Hakluyt's *The Principal Navigations Voyages Traffiques and Discoveries of the English Nation* in 1599 (Dharwadker 2003, 204). Muhammad's solo effort in expatriation was followed by the emergence of a host of writers on home soil: Raja Rammohun Roy (1772–1833), Henry Derozio (1809–31), Kashiprosad Ghose (1809–73), Kylas Chunder Dutt (1817–59), Michael Madhusudan Dutt (1827–73), Bankim Chandra Chatterjee (1838–94), Toru Dutt (1856–77), Rabindranath Tagore (1861–1941), and Rokeya Sakhawat Hossain (1880–1932). They were all Bengalis based in Calcutta (now Kolkata), as it was customary for wealthy, educated Bengalis, Hindu or Muslim, to settle in the city, which was then the capital of British India and the heartland of the region's commerce and culture.

However, from the above list, we know that Madhusudan Dutt and Rokeya Sakhawat Hossain were originally from places that now belong to Bangladesh: Dutt from Jessore district and Rokeya from Rangpur. Another writer in English, Humayun Kabir (1906–69), was from the Faridpur district of present-day Bangladesh. Therefore, it would not be too far-fetched to retrospectively claim these three writers as the pioneers of Bangladeshi anglophone literature.

Born in a rural area, Dutt moved at the age of eight to Calcutta, where his father was a prominent lawyer. He learnt Bangla, Sanskrit, and Persian in childhood and acquired English, Latin, and Hebrew at school. At 17, Dutt took up writing English poems and dreamed of travelling to England. In 1843, he converted to Christianity against his family's wishes, christened himself Michael, moved to Madras, and married a Scottish woman, Rebecca McTavish. He published his only book in English, a collection of three long poems, *The Captive Lady*, in 1849. In 1858, Dutt married a Frenchwoman, Henrietta, which proved to be a turning point in his career, as his new wife, "deeply enamoured of Bengal and the Bangla language" (Dharwadker 2003, 228), encouraged him to return to Bangla. Dutt made the transition in 1859, condemning his anglophone counterparts as "[s]warthy Macaulays and Carlyles and Thackerays" (Haq 2015, 4), and became one of the most celebrated writers in modern Bengali literature, comparable to Tagore and the national poet of Bangladesh, Kazi Nazrul Islam (1899–1976).

Rokeya Hossain was the first anglophone Muslim writer in Bengal and Bangladesh. Her famous feminist utopian satire, "Sultana's Dream", in which she created a Ladyland, turning the Indian androcentric world upside down by putting women at the helm of the state and relegating men to the inner quarters of the home, was published in the *Indian Ladies' Magazine* in 1905. She wrote two essays – "God Gives, Man Robs" and "Educational Ideals for the Modern Indian Girls" – and several letters in English. It is extraordinary that Rokeya, who had no formal education in childhood and was forbidden by her dogmatic father from learning the "un-Islamic" languages of English and Bangla, became one of the pioneering writers in the English language.

Humayan Kabir was the youngest Bengali-Bangladeshi anglophone writer of the colonial period. He was a brilliant student who obtained bachelor's and master's degrees in English literature from Calcutta University with first class and then moved to Oxford for further studies. Kabir was actively involved in the Oxford Union and was elected its secretary in 1930 and librarian in 1931. His first collection of English poetry, *Poems*, came out in 1932, and his novel, *Men and Rivers*, in 1945.

The anglophone tradition during the (East) Pakistan period

The paucity of Muslim names in the above list of anglophone writers indicates the negative attitude of Muslims, vis-à-vis Hindus, towards English at the time. The Muslim response to British rule and the English language differed radically from that of its *Brahmo* and Hindu counterparts. After their loss of power to the British, and particularly the replacement of Persian with English as India's official language in 1837, the Indian Muslim community became insular and indifferent to all affairs of the state. They saw the use of English as tantamount to a form of collaboration with the British rule that had replaced the Mughals. However, Hindus perceived British victory as "a deliverance [from] Muslim tyranny" (Chakraborty 2011, 76) and readily accepted English as a means of subduing their "inferior dissolute other" (77), the Muslims.

After the partition of 1947, the Pakistani regime sought to rectify this situation and adopt a more pragmatic view of English. It felt that there was more to benefit from retaining than rejecting the language, as sacrificing English might bring some temporary cultural victory but would involve relinquishing the many kinds of modern knowledge in science, technology, philosophy, and literature that came with it. Besides, given the country's linguistic ecology, in which all its provinces have their regional languages, such as Bangla, Punjabi, Sindhi, and Baluchi, English could act as a conduit among this diverse population and help in bringing the nation together. Moreover, the local languages would benefit from interactions with English, as languages do when allowed to coexist in a benign contact zone. With such constructive views in mind, English was retained as one of Pakistan's official languages and used in different spheres of everyday life such as education and administration.

This changing scenario created a wholesome environment for English and aspiring writers in the language. However, to sort out the linguistic gap between the different provinces and ethnicities and enhance national unity and harmony, the Pakistani authorities adopted another policy move, which threatened not only the future of English, especially in East Pakistan, but also the very existence of the federation. At a public rally at Ramna Race Course (Suhrawardy Udyan) in Dhaka on March 21, 1948, the founder and then Governor-General of Pakistan, Muhammad Ali Jinnah, unequivocally declared Urdu the only state language of Pakistan, a view he reiterated at a gathering of students at the University of Dhaka on March 24, 1948. This created an outcry among the Bengalis of East

Pakistan. The ruling elites of West Pakistan thought that Bengalis in East Pakistan would accept Urdu as the nation's lingua franca as it was putatively symbolic of Muslim culture, in a manner similar to Sanskrit in Hindu culture. However, East Pakistani Bengalis could not fathom why they would have to sacrifice their mother tongue for an alien language, given that they formed the country's majority population. This fuelled enough anger and resentment among East Pakistanis to start a language movement (*Bhasha Andolon*) that gathered further steam after the killing of several students by the police at a political rally in Dhaka on February 21, 1952[2] and eventually led to the dissolution of Pakistan and the formation of the new nation-state of Bangladesh in 1971.

This movement, although directed against Urdu, made the people of East Pakistan so parochial and inward-looking in their identity that they rejected all foreign languages, including English, in an effort to bolster their mother tongue. This nationalist ferment created a hostile environment for promising writers in English in East Pakistan. If they wrote in languages other than Bangla, they were made to feel contrite or threatened. Notwithstanding this oppressive milieu, English writing made some headway during the period, maintaining a somewhat subdued and veiled presence. The notable writers of the period include Nirad Chaudhuri (1897–1999), Syed Waliullah (1922–71), Ganesh Bagchi (1926–), and Sayeed Ahmed (1931–2010) – almost all of whom wrote under two flags, Pakistan and Bangladesh, and in both English and Bangla.

Among these writers, Chaudhuri is the most renowned. Of his many books, *The Autobiography of an Unknown Indian* (1951) is considered a masterpiece but also controversial as it was dedicated to the memory of the British Empire. His fellow literati ostracized him for his open advocacy for European culture and contempt for India. Partly because of this controversy, he left East Pakistan and settled in Oxford, where he was awarded an honorary doctorate by the University of Oxford in 1990 and an honorary CBE by Queen Elizabeth II in 1992. Bagchi also left the country – first for India and then Uganda. He published his collection of plays, *The Deviant*, and a second volume, *Of Malice and Men*, both in 1968. His autobiographical novel, *No Room for Love*, came out in 1999, and his autobiography, *My Days and Ways*, in 2014.

Ahmed was a playwright and deemed the pioneer of the theatre of the absurd in Bangladeshi literature. He wrote three plays in English: *The Thing* (1961), *Milepost* (1965), and *Survival* (1966). Waliullah was a prolific writer in Bangla but also produced several English works. His first English novel, *The Ugly Asian*, came out in 1958, and *Tree Without Roots*, a transcreation of his earlier Bangla classic *Lalshalu* (1948), was published in 1967. He also wrote two short stories in English, "The Escape" and "No Enemy" (both published in the 1950s), and has left behind an unfinished novel manuscript, oddly titled *How to Cook Beans*.

Anglophone literature in post-independence Bangladesh

English writing was already in a diminished and desultory state before independence, but it almost disappeared from Bangladesh's linguistic and literary milieu in the immediate years after independence. This was mainly because of the violent circumstances in which the country was born. Bangladesh came into being in 1971 after a nine-month-long *muktijuddho*, or War of Liberation, in which the Pakistani forces committed heinous ethnic cleansing, mass murder, and genocidal rape. By some estimates, 269,000 Bengalis, including many leading intellectuals of the country, were killed, and 200,000 women were raped during this war ("269,000 People Died" 2008). After paying such a tremendous price for their mother tongue and motherland, it is no surprise that English became a pariah language, phased out of everyday life and Bangla was consecrated as the sole medium of education and administration in post-independence Bangladesh. Even the few English-medium schools in the major urban centres that acted as seedbeds for anglophone writing were converted to the Bangla medium. In that blinkered atmosphere, any creative activity other than Bangla was considered anathema, and militant nationalists regarded anyone going against the grain as a freak or traitor.

English and English writing dwindled for another reason: the country's linguistic composition. As mentioned earlier, Pakistan comprises multiple ethnicities and languages, and the same is true for India, which has "23 official languages, spoken in different parts of the country" ("Languages in India" n.d.). Given such polylingual diversity, English enjoys an aura of "cultural neutrality" (Rushdie 1997, xi) in both countries, helping in interethnic dialogues, even to the point that, as Rushdie contends, "[i]n many parts of South India, people [...] prefer to converse with visiting North Indians in English rather than Hindi" (xi). However, that potential role of English in the nation-building process was unwarranted in Bangladesh as it is a largely monolingual society, with, as M. Obaidul Hamid and Md. Mahmudul Hasan (2020) affirm, "98 percent of [its] people speak[ing] Bangla or its regional dialects" (297).

Notwithstanding the exaltation of Bangla and exclusion of English from national affairs, English writing continued to flow in a thin, slow stream, mainly by those groomed in English-medium schools during the Pakistani era. Prominent among these writers are Razia Khan, Kaiser Haq, Niaz Zaman, and Adib Khan; the first of these wrote both poetry and fiction, the second excelled in poetry, and the remaining two made their names in fiction. Except for Razia Khan, who passed away in 2011, these writers are still active and maintain a strong presence in the anglophone literary scene, with Haq and Zaman writing from home and Khan from Australia.

Razia Khan, a decorated writer in Bangla, commenced writing in English in the early 1950s. However, her two volumes of poetry, *Argus under Anaesthesia* and *Cruel April*, came out in 1976 and 1977 respectively. She also wrote two novels, *The Enchanted Delta* and *The Tamarind Tree*, both published posthumously in 2020. Her works generally focus on gender, nationalism, and multiculturalism, expressing a deep sense of pride in Bangladeshi history, culture, and identity and a call for the empowerment of women.

Haq, a student and later colleague of Razia Khan at the University of Dhaka and arguably the most internationally acclaimed Bangladeshi poet in English, embarked on his poetic career in the late 1960s, inspired by Brother Hobart, his literature teacher at school, and by D.H. Lawrence's poem "Snake" (Haq 1997, 113). Haq's first two poetry volumes, *Starting Lines: Poems 1968–1975* and *A Little Ado*, came out in 1978. He has since published six more titles, including two collected editions: *Published in the Streets of Dhaka: Collected Poems* (2007) and *Pariah and Other Poems* (2013).

Writer and activist Niaz Zaman has published three novels and three collections of short stories. Her debut novel, *The Crooked Neem Tree* (1982), made her the first acknowledged anglophone novelist in the post-independence period. Her other two novels, *A Different Sita* and *The Baromashi Tapes*, came out in 2011. Her short story collections include *The Dance and Other Stories* (1996), *Didima's Necklace and Other Stories* (2005), and *The*

Maidens' Club (2015). Zaman (2021) highlights a critical problem for female writers in a conservative society like Bangladesh when she explains in an interview that men have the freedom to write about any subject, but women have to be discerning because "[p]eople will not say anything about male writers, but they will defame a woman" (264).

Adib Khan is a transnational writer and the first Bangladeshi to win international awards. His first novel, *Seasonal Adjustments* (1994), set in Australia and Bangladesh, received the Christina Stead Prize for Fiction, the Book of the Year award in the 1994 NSW Premier's Literary Awards, and the 1995 Commonwealth Writers' Prize for Best First Book. He has since published four more novels, set in Australia, Bangladesh, India, and Vietnam: *Solitude of Illusions* (1996), *The Story Teller* (2000), *Homecoming* (2003), and *Spiral Road* (2007).

The situation with English and English writing began to change in the 1990s as the memory of the Liberation War gradually began to recede in the national psyche, and Bangladeshis came to recognize the importance of English as the emerging global language and the language of digital and information technology. With the advent of the Internet, satellite television, and social media, English began to penetrate widely and deeply into society, and it was no longer possible to look the other way. Therefore, English was reintroduced in government schools as a compulsory subject at all levels, and private English schools and universities began to proliferate in the major cities. As a result, English once again became a language of opportunity and status and the de facto second language in urban areas, although, paradoxically, it still had no official recognition or acknowledgement in the country's Constitution.

To bring Bangladesh to the world and open up opportunities for young aspiring anglophone writers through interactions with those from abroad, a new literary festival in English, the Dhaka Hay Festival, was launched in 2011. It began as a trial at the British Council precinct on the Dhaka University campus but has since become a major literary event after it was rebranded as the Dhaka Literature Festival and relocated to the Bangla Academy – the custodian of Bangla language, literature, and culture – in 2014. This move marked a symbolic victory for English as it was coexisting with the national language for the first time. It also showed an acceptance by the establishment that an uptick for English was not necessarily a downtick for Bangla but rather an opportunity for both languages to flourish through reciprocity and cross-fertilization, transcending the discourse of animosity and binarism.

However, despite such positive developments, writers in English still face considerable challenges. For example, there is still no proper literary infrastructure for English writing. No reputable international publishing houses operate in the country, and a few boutique publishers who cater to local writers lack professional vetting, editing, and marketing facilities to ensure quality. Moreover, books (English or Bangla) published in Bangladesh hardly ever cross the border, even to India. This is a huge impediment to the growth of English writing in Bangladesh. It prevents writers from reaching and cultivating a global readership and building their international reputation. The readership cohort inside the country is also limited mainly to the students and graduates of the English departments. Besides, the quality of literary criticism is not up to standard, as only a handful of Bangladeshi critics have so far succeeded in publishing about the country's anglophone writers in internationally recognized journals. What is more, Bangladeshi university curricula are old-fashioned and mimic the colonial model; very few, if any, local anglophone writers are ever taught in the classroom to foster and incentivize a homegrown anglophone literary tradition.

Yet, with the changing scenario, Bangladeshi writers are publishing at a continually increasing rate both at home and abroad, though more of them are established overseas. Most write fiction, and many have published only one book. The most prominent among these new writers are Monica Ali, Tahmima Anam, Zia Haider Rahman, Dilruba Z. Ara, Mahmud Rahman, Neamat Imam, K. Anis Ahmed, Ruby Zaman, and Shazia Omar – all of whom work in the genre of fiction.

British Bangladeshi writer Monica Ali is perhaps the most renowned in this millennium cohort for her successful inaugural novel *Brick Lane* (2003). She has since published three more fictional works, including, most recently, *Love Marriage* (2022), a riveting story about British multiculturalism, narrated in a rich, witty, and sensitive style.

Tahmima Anam, Zia Haider Rahman, Dilruba Z. Ara, Mahmud Rahman, and Neamat Imam are all non-resident writers, while K. Anis Ahmed, Ruby Zaman, and Shazia Omar live in Bangladesh. Anam, domiciled in the UK, is the author of four novels, a trilogy – *A Golden Age* (2007), *The Good Muslim* (2011), and *The Bones of Grace* (2016) – and *The Startup Wife* (2021). Her first novel, which explores the history of the Liberation War, won the Commonwealth Writers' Prize for Best First Book in 2008. Zia Haider Rahman, another British Bangladeshi writer, also probes the Liberation War in his only novel, *In the Light of What We Know* (2014). Winner of the James Tait Black Memorial Prize, this work was praised by Joyce Carol Oates (2014) as "a novel of ideas, a compendium of epiphanies, paradoxes, and riddles clearly designed to be read slowly and meditatively". Ara, Mahmud Rahman, and Imam live in Sweden, the US, and Canada respectively.

Ara is the author of two novels and a collection of short stories: *A List of Offences* (2006), *Blame* (2015), and *Detached Belonging* (2016). Rahman has published a collection of short stories focusing on the effects of war, migration, and cultural dislocation, *Killing the Water* (2010). Imam's only novel to date is *The Black Coat* (2013), depicting the political crisis in the wake of independence, for which he controversially blames Sheik Mujib, the Father of the Nation.

Among those writing from home, Ahmed has a collection of short stories, *Mr. Kissinger and Other Stories* (2012), and a novel, *The World in My Hands* (2013); Ruby Zaman, a novel, *Invisible Lines* (2011); and Omar, a short story collection, *Like a Diamond in the Sky* (2010), and a fictional narrative, *Dark Diamond* (2016).

Poetry has not fared as well and lags far behind the fiction genre. Nevertheless, some accomplishments deserve mention. These include, among those writing from home, Sofiul Azam's *Impasse* (2003), *In Love with Gorgon* (2010), and *Safe Under Water* (2014); Sadaf Saaz's *Sari Reams* (2013); Shamsad Mortuza's *Barkode* (2013); and M. Shafiqul Islam's *Inner State* (2020). Notable works by diasporic poets include Tarifa Faizullah's *Seam* (2014) and *Registers of Illuminated Villages* (2018), and Nausheen Eusuf's chapbook *What Remains* (2011) and the full-length collection *Not Elegy, But Eros* (2017), which contains a Pushcart Prize-winning poem.

Bangladeshi literature in English has made considerable progress since its inception in the colonial period. It went through a semi-muzzled period during the East Pakistan era and the early decades of the country's political reincarnation as Bangladesh. However, there has been a surge of activity in the new millennium, with several writers making breakthroughs in the international literary scene and winning prestigious prizes. If this trend continues, the tradition promises a bright future, although to catch up with its South Asian neighbours, it needs more speed and energy to make up for the lost ground. A second observation, as hinted earlier, is that the tradition seems to be growing more rapidly in the diaspora than at home. To address this imbalance and to create a vibrant anglophone literary site at home, the country's leadership needs to take appropriate measures to strengthen the state of English and its literary fabric. A robust English writing tradition will help bring Bangladesh closer to the world by sharing its history and culture with people of other countries in the global lingua franca, something that cannot be achieved if the national spirit is invested wholly in Bangla.

To introduce this tradition to international readers and researchers of postcolonial literature, we have included five articles and two interviews in this book. In the first of these articles, "Muslim Bengal writes back: Rokeya's encounter with and representation of Europe", Md. Mahmudul Hasan examines how, despite its exploitative nature, colonialism facilitated continuous cultural exchanges between Muslim Bengal, home of the writer Rokeya Sakhawat Hossain, and the European metropolis. Although Rokeya never visited Europe, she was exposed to European literature and engaged in a sophisticated critique and assessment of European culture in relation to her own environment. The article explores the ways in which, as a writer, educationalist, activist, and wife of a civil servant, Rokeya had opportunities to interact directly with European women and indirectly with European men. Importantly, she made available to her readers an interpretative summary of Marie Corelli's novel *The Murder of Delicia* (1896), informed them about the Victorian "woman question", and identified comparable gender norms in Europe and India. The article discusses how Rokeya broke through the iron gate of purdah practices prevalent at the time, availed herself of opportunities to explore European culture, and commented on the condition of women both in Britain and Muslim Bengal that includes what is now Bangladesh.

In the second article, "Panchayat and colonialism in Humayun Kabir's *Men and Rivers*", also by Hasan, the author discusses the earliest significant English-language novel written by a pre-independence pioneer of the tradition by situating the book's narrative in its historical background and within postcolonial discourse. As Kabir's treatment of the colonial theme in *Men and Rivers* is implicit, Hasan attempts a detailed textual and contextual reading of the novel in order to locate its setting in British colonial Bengal. Drawing upon Frantz Fanon's dialectic of decolonization and liberation, he foregrounds the novel in contemporary peasant movements led by A.K. Fazlul Huq and Maulana Abdul Hamid Khan Bhashani and shows the importance of the peasantry in Bengal's socio-economic structure. The discussion of the novel focuses on a specific aspect of peasant life – the indigenous panchayat system – which is contrasted with colonial rule in a way that highlights the egalitarian character of the former and the exploitive nature in which the colonizer applied economic and cultural force upon innocent peasants. The article ends by pointing to Kabir's cosmopolitan credentials and, at the same time, his rootedness and interest in East Bengal peasant society.

In the third article, '"Here I'll stay': Kaiser Haq's poems and the impact of being at home", Kathryn Hummel investigates the sense of both physical and emotional rootedness in Haq's poetry. Even though one cannot avoid the impact of temporal and cultural homelessness or diaspora, Hummel looks at Haq's poetry through the lens of his physical presence in Bangladesh, from which he understands and interacts with the outside world. Referring to a range of Haq's poems, she sees his sense of physicality as dynamic and developing (not static and predetermined), regards him as a "transnational local", and associates him with identities that are not easy to pigeonhole or stereotype. However, Hummel shows that Haq's situatedness in Dhaka is manifested in some poems that deal with contemporary, local issues.

In the fourth article, "Toxic grace?: Tahmima Anam's *The Bones of Grace* and the pollution trade", Md. Alamgir Hossain explores the last novel of Anam's Bengal trilogy in light of environmental degradation and risks to human life that stem from pollution migration from rich (polluting) to poor (polluted) countries – all in the name of development under the aegis of neo-liberal globalization. As the novel is partly set in the coastal zone of Chittagong, Bangladesh's leading ship-breaking site, the article elaborates on the deleterious effects of global capitalist penetration in countries like Bangladesh on environmental subalterns who are the ultimate recipients of pollution burdens coming from the Global North. Exploring the relationships between literature and environment as depicted in Anam's novel, Hossain questions the conventional notion of development and seeks to redefine it in line with the interest of the Global South and its ecology in order to thwart (environmental) injustices wrought by global (northern) capitalism's corporate greed.

In "Beyond national(ist) binaries: The case of Zia Haider Rahman's *In the Light of What We Know*", the fifth article, Md Rezaul Haque examines a sensitive nationalist issue described in Rahman's debut novel. Because of the dark history of relations between Bangladesh and Pakistan associated with the War of Liberation discussed earlier, a Manichean divide seemingly exists between the populations of these two erstwhile wings of united Pakistan. The vantage point of the diasporic third space provides Rahman with a degree of detachment and objectivity, enabling him to see post-1971 affairs between the two countries through a new lens. Haque capitalizes on this to contest the jingoistic emotionalism and parochial rhetoric emanating from the nationalist discourses of Bangladesh and Pakistan. The article anticipates a relationship of mutual respect, friendship, and shared understanding between the two countries – an agenda Rahman fictionally sets up in his novel.

In "Introducing a Bangladeshi writer in English: An interview with Kaiser Haq", the first of the two interviews, a post-independence first-generation anglophone poet deliberates on the challenges and prospects of the tradition before the new millennium and explains why he feels sceptical about its future. He also relates how he caught the creative writing bug in English, the major influences on his imagination, and how he views the country's political lay of the land. Moreover, Haq explains his relationship with Bangla and Bangla literature, Subcontinental English, the Indo-Anglian tradition, and humour. He recollects his experience as a Bangladesh Liberation War veteran and his contribution as a well-known translator of Bangla literature into English.

Finally, in "Delving beneath the surface: An interview with Monica Ali", the second interview, Sadaf Saaz conducts a conversation with arguably the most prominent second-generation Bangladeshi writer in English. In it, Ali speaks candidly about issues related to her latest novel *Love Marriage* (2022), especially the cultural hybridity that is at work in the microcosm of multicultural families in contemporary Britain, which, according to her, is perhaps comparable to Jane Austen's perceptions of inter-class relations in marriage. She also touches on her shift from the monocultural in her debut novel, *Brick Lane*, to the transcultural in *Love Marriage*. Other topics addressed in the interview include Ali's writing process, her purpose in writing, the experience of her dual heritage, her thoughts on feminism, and her assessment of the place of class and race in today's Britain.

Notes

1. Bengal was divided for the first time in 1905, but it lasted only for six years because of the mounting protests by the elite Hindus of West Bengal led by, among others, Rabindranath Tagore. His patriotic songs galvanized the Bengalis to fight for reunification, and one of his songs composed during this movement later became the national anthem of Bangladesh. However, the map created in 1905 to separate Muslim-majority East Bengal from Hindu-majority West Bengal was adopted to create East Pakistan during the partition of 1947, and the same map now marks the national boundary of Bangladesh.
2. This day was declared the International Mother Language Day by UNESCO in 2002.

Disclosure statement

No potential conflict of interest was reported by the authors.

ORCID

Mohammad A. Quayum http://orcid.org/0000-0002-3159-023X
Md. Mahmudul Hasan http://orcid.org/0000-0001-5170-2406

References

"269,000 People died in Bangladesh war, says new study." 2008. *The Times of India*, June 20. https://timesofindia.indiatimes.com/world/rest-of-world/269000-people-died-in-Bangladesh-war-says-new-study/articleshow/3147513.cms.

Chakraborty, Rachana. 2011. "Beginning of Muslim Women's Education in Colonial Bengal." *History and Research* 1 (1): 75–88.

Dharwadker, Vinay. 2003. "The Historical Formation of Indian-English Literature." In *Literary Cultures in History: Reconstructions from South Asia*, edited by Sheldon Pollock, 199–270. Berkeley, CA: University of California Press.

Hamid, M. Obaidul, and Md. Mahmudul Hasan. 2020. "Bangladeshi English." In *The Handbook of Asian Englishes*, edited by Kingsley Bolton, Werner Botha, and Andy Kirkpatrick, 297–315. Hoboken, NJ: John Wiley and Sons.

Haq, Kaiser. 1997. "Introducing a Bangladeshi Writer in English: Interview with Kaiser Haq [M.A. Quayum]." *World Literature Written in English* 36 (1): 110–119. doi:10.1080/ 17449859708589266.

Haq, Kaiser. 2015. "The Hijra Comes in from the Heat and Dust: Notes Towards a Definition of Bangladeshi Writing in English." *Wasafiri* 30 (4): 3–7. doi:10.1080/02690055.2015.1068982.

"Languages of India." n.d. *New World Encyclopedia*. Accessed 26 June 2022. www.newworldencyclopedia.org/entry/Languages_of_India.

Mukherjee, Meenakshi. 1971. *The Twice Born Fiction: Themes and Techniques of the Indian Novel in English*. New Delhi: Heinemann.

Oates, Joyce Carol. 2014. "'Witness to the Unknowable'. Review of *in the Light of What We Know*, by Zia Haider Rahman." *The New York Review*, October 23. www.nybooks.com/articles/ 2014/10/23/witness-unknowable-zia-haider-rahman/.

Rushdie, Salman. 1997. "Introduction." In *Mirrorwork: 50 Years of Indian Writing 1947–1997*, edited by Salman Rushdie and Elizabeth West, vii–xx. New York: Henry Holt and Company.

Zaman, Niaz. 2021. "A Multi-Talented Writer: An Interview with Niaz Zaman [Jackie Kabir]." In *Bangladeshi Literature in English: A Critical Anthology*, edited by Mohammad A. Quayum and Md. Mahmudul Hasan, 258–269. Dhaka: Asiatic Society of Bangladesh.

Muslim Bengal writes back: Rokeya's encounter with and representation of Europe

Md. Mahmudul Hasan

ABSTRACT
Despite its exploitative nature, colonialism facilitated continuous cultural exchanges between Muslim Bengal, home of the writer Rokeya Sakhawat Hossain, and the European metropolis. Although Rokeya never visited Europe, she was exposed to European literature, overcame sociocultural constraints, and thus became engaged in a complex critique and assessment of European culture in relation to her own environment. This article explores the ways in which, as a writer, educationalist, activist and wife of a civil servant, Rokeya had opportunities to interact directly with European women and indirectly with European men. Importantly, she made available to her readers an interpretative summary of Marie Corelli's novel *The Murder of Delicia* (1896), informed them about the Victorian "woman question" and identified comparable gender norms in Europe and India. This article discusses how Rokeya broke through the iron gate of purdah practices prevalent at the time, availed herself of opportunities to explore European culture, and commented on the condition of women.

Introduction

Rokeya Sakhawat Hossain (1880–1932) is the most prominent 20th-century Muslim woman writer from what is now Bangladesh. On both political and intellectual fronts, she fought for women's right to education, equal franchise and participation in public life and against their incarceration in the home and social and legal discrimination. Because of her concern for women's rights and equal opportunities, she is often regarded as a "feminist" author, although the term was not widely used in her lifetime, and she never attached it to her name. In Bangladesh, she is unanimously recognized as the voice and spirit of her time and beyond and is highly esteemed as a visionary social reformer; hence, the honorific term "begum" is prefixed to her name and she is popularly known as Begum Rokeya.[1]

At the time of Rokeya's active creative career, British India was a meeting place for Indian and European people.[2] However, the gradual, persistent incursion of a western-dominated economy and subsequent colonial exploitation resulted in the growth of Indian nationalist sentiment originating mainly in Rokeya's Bengal: the Swadeshi movement, which advocated principally the support of local industries using home-produced materials, such as cotton, and the boycott of foreign goods, most of which were imported from Europe. Such a politico-economic context triggered a nationalist literature that "sought to define a native identity different from European constructions of the same" (Nayar 2008), as it was believed that "instilling a national consciousness would first require establishing a common enemy (the European) and a common cultural denominator" (41). Since an intense anti-colonial nationalist struggle was gaining momentum, the relation between the Europeans and colonized people was further strained, and the two groups maintained a degree of social, political and psychological distance. E.M. Forster's *A Passage to India* (1924) creatively explores "white paranoia and hysteria" and the "fear of the colonial Other" (Friedman 2005, 250). In Bengal, European colonizers, who heavily influenced the dominant culture, displayed a deep-seated resistance to pluralism or to the possibility of mutual interaction and negotiation between the colonial masters and their Indian subjects.

In such a highly charged political context, Rokeya struck a balance in addressing issues of women's liberation from patriarchy and India's independence from British colonial rule and at the same time, as an individual, engaging in intellectual encounters with Europeans and benefitting from cultural and linguistic diversity. Like some of her British counterparts, she acted as a cultural bridge between Muslim Bengal and England. Since Rokeya is a pre-independence writer who lived in a politico-cultural climate of heightened consciousness, an exploration of the various aspects of her encounter with European colonialism, and her perceptions of Europe, provides a significant perspective on the heterogeneous dynamics of the colonial contact zone of Bengal, and its social patterns.

Keeping this cultural context in view, this article will investigate how, as a pioneering figure in the literary and cultural history of Muslim Bengal, Rokeya imagined and represented Europe. Feminist concerns and a strong urge for the betterment of her society span a broad spectrum of her writing. However, in this article I will touch upon specific works from her oeuvre that contain European characters or refer to the colonizers' presence in India. I will go on to discuss Rokeya's understanding of the plot and themes of Marie Corelli's novel *The Murder of Delicia* (1896) and how in her adaptation she transforms the text and reflects the main ideas of the original, relating its message to the sociocultural conditions of women in India. I will also examine Rokeya's short play *Shourajagot* to show how she perceived her Bengal and Corelli's England as maintaining comparable socially constructed gender norms and differences. Such a comparative analysis sheds new light on the similarities between Rokeya's and Corelli's depiction of women's condition and cultural circumstances, as well as highlighting commonalities in the two writers' feminist stance.

Before engaging in analysis of these texts, it is necessary to contextualize Rokeya's encounter with Europe, as it occurred in the colonial setting of Bengal. She did not travel to Europe to gather first-hand experiences. Accordingly, her representation of Europe is largely dependent on her reading of European material, and personal interactions and experiences with Europeans living in India, as well as on her imaginative verve, intelligent curiosity and amazing scholarly resourcefulness, creative energy and insights. Therefore, her representation of the continent and its culture combines both realistic and imaginative elements.

Colonial cultural engagements

Just as Indian and British societies are blended in Rokeya's writing, in the real world there were constant cultural and official communications between Europe and the Indian subcontinent. Colonial officials and educationists, as well as literary figures from England, would travel to the British Indian Empire for diplomatic, administrative, educational and other purposes. Their wives gave birth to children, some of whom later became renowned figures of English literature. For example, William Makepeace Thackeray (1811–63), Rudyard Kipling (1865–1936) and George Orwell (1903–50) were all born in India, and Kipling and Orwell were contemporaries of Rokeya who lived in and wrote about Indian society and culture. E.M. Forster (1879–1970) made extensive visits to British India and, as has been noted, commented perceptively on the colonial relationship between the British and Indians. Earlier, the writer Edmund Burke (1729–97) had made speeches in the British parliament against the colonial oppression of the East India Company under Warren Hastings (1732–1818). Burke "argue[d] that the unjust and exploitative economic policies of the East India Company, under the leadership of Warren Hastings, […] led to the devastation of both the common and noble families of India" (Botting 2006, 80). So the cultural engagement of British writers with India had already spanned two centuries, as these writers creatively fed the European readership with images of Indian life, acting as cultural bridges between the metropolis and the colony – a role Rokeya played as an Indian counterpart to European writers by way of informing her compatriots about the cultural content and structure of Europe, even though she never visited the continent.

English writers influenced Rokeya's contemporary Indian writers and reformers. Raja Rammohan Roy (1772–1833) was a friend of Jeremy Bentham and of Robert Owen, and read James Mill's celebrated work *History of India* (1818; Murshid 1983, 23). Satyendranath Tagore (1842–1923) is said to have been influenced by J.S. Mill's *Subjection of Women* (1869) in his ideas concerning women's liberation, since a generation of educated Indians was "influenced by the thoughts of J.S. Mill and Spencer. They accepted the utilitarian ethics coupled with empiricist rationalism" (Deshpande, Paranjpe, Shrikant, Raja, and Das 1997, 121). Keshub Chandra Sen (1838–84), the Hindu philosopher, social reformer and founder of the Brahma Samaj of India, made acquaintances with English writers. He was influenced by "Victorian ideas of social reform" (Amin 1996, 83), and his correspondence and debate with the English Unitarian and educationalist Annette Akroyd (1842–1929) concerning girls' education is common knowledge.

Thus the systematic intercultural exchanges and fusions generated by colonial conditions suggest that the material atmosphere of Rokeya's society provided ample scope for a writer to interact with and benefit from western intellectuals. In other words, even though the rigid purdah system impeded women's movement in public life and denied them interactions with men outside their own family, the overall social and cultural context of the time provided Rokeya with many means by which to read and become familiar with European writers.

Rokeya's exposure to Europe and interactions with Europeans

Through political machinations and military manoeuvres, the British colonizers had taken over India from Muslim rulers; they subsequently marginalized the Muslim community in almost all areas of the public domain. As a result, Muslims felt doubly dispossessed and subordinated and, compared to the relationship between other native communities and Europeans, their engagement and interaction with the latter stationed in India was relatively disadvantaged and unenthusiastic. Like other pre-independence writers, Rokeya experienced the obtrusive presence of colonial administrators and intellectuals in her country. She was well aware of the systematic marginalization and neglect of her fellow Muslims by both the colonizers and the dominant Hindu community (Hossain [1973] 2006, 229).

The colonialist narrative, especially as represented in William Wilson Hunter's book *Indian Mussalmans* (1871), sought to depict the Muslim community as "inherently hostile to British rule" and to keep "the elite Muslim[s]" away from nationalist sentiment and thus render them politically irrelevant (Sarkar 2008, 140). A subsequent, growing communal divide led Hindu chauvinists, especially those in Bengal, to characterize Muslims as "foreign invaders", "ex-Hindu converts" and "traitors" (Sarkar 2008, 142). As a result, while British colonial marginalization of Muslims was obvious, there was always a fear among Muslims that even if India became independent, they "would be oppressed under a representative system in which Hindus would be in a majority" (Brass 2000, 887). In such a context of uncertainty, for Muslims there were psychological barriers of antagonism, suspicion and fear that militated against any unhindered social and cultural communications with Europeans. Furthermore, as mentioned earlier, the scope of Rokeya's intellectual exchange was rigidly curtailed by traditional practices of purdah or seclusion of women from men and even to some extent from non-related women (Hossain ([1973] 2006, 395–397) as well as by the colonizers' tendency to maintain a distance between themselves and the colonized.

As well as interacting with Europeans, Rokeya would have come to know about Europe through formal English education. However, Muslims were generally opposed to this educational system – an attitude Rokeya critiques, believing that this attitude rendered their children socially and politically less competitive and economically less viable in comparison with other sections of the community (Hossain [1973] 2006, 491). While most Muslims considered western education as out of bounds, privileged parents like Rokeya's father sent their sons to colonial educational institutions for European learning. However, because of the pseudo-religious and cultural stance against female education and the social stigma attached to it, he did not send any of his daughters to school. Moreover, sites of higher learning like St Xavier's College in Calcutta founded in 1860 – which his sons attended – admitted only male students. Such colleges in British India were founded mainly by Roman Catholics who did not open any women's colleges "until the twentieth century" (Dinakarlal 2014, 118).

Muslim women's access to European education and cultural products was doubly restricted, because of their gender and religious identity. The colonial administration "established an educational institution for girls, Bethune School, in Calcutta in 1849 (later developed into the Bethune College in 1879); but access for Muslim girls was restricted until 1885" (Hasan 2013, 45). Equal educational opportunities for Muslim girls came about only in 1939 with the opening of Lady Brabourne College, founded "mainly – but not exclusively – for Muslim girls" (Amin 1996, xiii). So, like most other Muslim women of her time, Rokeya did not have the opportunity to receive a formal, western education.

Even though she disapproved of prevalent domestic gender norms and contested the extreme nature of purdah, Rokeya complied with these practices, mainly to minimize the risk of male antagonism to her agenda of female education and other measures of women's empowerment. However, that did not stop her from developing forms of intellectual and intercultural communication with Europeans, since historically "there has been a myriad of strong and independent Muslim women, veiled and unveiled, who have broken down projected dichotomies between public and private" (Lambert-Hurley 2007a, 2). Rokeya's assertion about women's spatial freedom is unambiguous: "Many people do not understand that in the Muslim religion it is allowed (for woman) to travel home and abroad maintaining scripture-sanctioned purdah" (Hossain [1973] 2006, 189).

Rokeya's contemporary Sarojini Naidu (1879–1949) was educated at "King's College of the University of London and then at Girton, though without taking a degree" (Roy 1998, 132), and was imbued with the feminist, suffragist spirit. Other contemporaries, such as "Pandita Ramabai [1858–1922], Cornelia Sorabji [1866–1954], and Rukhmabai [1864–1955], traveled to Britain in search of further education" (Burton 1994, 8). For Muslim women, the journey has been a notable aspect of their life and an essential component of their religious observance, as "every Muslim, male and female, must make a scripted visit to the Ka'aba in Mecca during the assigned month of D[h]ill-Hijja at least once in their lifetime, if they can afford it" (Lambert-Hurley 2007b, vii). Rokeya makes references to hajj in order to reject the Indian notion of restricting women's movement and appearance in public (Hossain [1973] 2006, 251–252).

Lambert-Hurley provides an account of "counterflow to colonialism" and argues that "South Asian Muslims, whether male or female, were enabled by established patterns of movement within the Islamic world to go abroad in larger numbers and with greater ease than many of their fellow Indians" (2007b, xiii, xiv). The famous begums of Bhopal – Nawab Qudsiya Begum (r. 1819–37), Sikandar Begum (1819–68), Shah Jahan Begum (1838–1901) and Sultan Jahan Begum (1858–1930) – were great travellers. Sultan Jahan Begum travelled extensively in Britain and donated money to build a masjid in Woking, Surrey; it takes its name, Shah Jahan Mosque, from her. Atiya Fyzee (1877–1967) travelled to Europe in 1906–07, had "the opportunity to observe European culture and society more generally" and interacted "with an impressive array of highly influential British and Indian reformers, politicians, and intellectuals" (Lambert-Hurley and Sharma 2010, 1). In 1941, nine years after Rokeya's death, a later Muslim woman writer from Calcutta, politician-diplomat Shaista Ikramullah (1915–2000) completed a PhD at the University of London. Equally, as part of "cultural imperialism", there was a continuous series of "voyages out" by British women – such as Lady Dufferin (1843–1935), Margaret Elizabeth Noble (known as Sister Nivedita; 1867–1911) and Margaret Cousins (1878–1954) – who journeyed to British India for "zenana teaching" and for other purposes, while feminists in the metropolis, like Elizabeth Adelaide Manning (1828–1905) and Millicent Fawcett (1847–1929), took an interest in Indian women's issues (Burton 1994, 26–27). Importantly, in 1893, the socialist, suffragette and theosophist Annie Besant (1847–1933) moved to British India for good. She established the Indian Home Rule League in 1916, strove for the welfare of the colonized Indians and their country's independence, and defied internment by the British authorities (Aiyar 1963, 71–72).

The discussion above suggests the "complex nature of cultural encounters" (Lambert-Hurley 2007b, lxi) in British India, in particular the Victorian woman question, from which Rokeya may have benefitted in terms of understanding Europe. She interacted with Europeans living in India and imaginatively journeyed through the continent by means of books, and her depiction of Europe and Europeans blends realism with imaginative fantasy and intuitive interpretation.

Significantly, Rokeya communicated with English colleagues of her husband, befriending and closely interacting with Europeans such as Lady Chelmsford, Annie Besant and Mr McPherson (Hasan 2013, 54). Deeply involved in educational activities, working day in and day out, running Sakhawat Memorial Girls' School, she came into contact with, and received visits from, European officials of the education department, as well as prominent British personalities, particularly those who came to the colony for educational purposes.

Rokeya's geographical affiliations were also enabling factors in her learning about European culture. She was born in Rangpur, and after marriage followed her husband to various places in India, briefly living in Bhagalpur after his death and finally settling down in Calcutta. After the British had defeated Nawab Sirajuddaula (the last sovereign ruler of Bengal) at the Battle of Palashi on 23 June 1757 (and subsequently murdered him), they captured Calcutta and switched from indirect domination to direct colonial rule. Calcutta became increasingly important "after 1765, when the East India Company had acquired the diwani of Bengal" (Mann 2004, 31). In 1772 the capital of Bengal was moved from Murshidabad, 100 miles south to Calcutta, and from then Calcutta was the capital of British India until 1912, when "the British […] installed themselves in their imperial capital at New Delhi" (Inden 1990, 148). So, for nearly a century-and-a-half, Calcutta was the centre of the British administration, with the result that Bengal was more exposed to western influences than other parts of India. Since Rokeya lived in Calcutta all through her active writing career and was hugely involved in its intellectual culture, she had the opportunity to interact with Europeans and to read western materials imported from the metropolis.

After her marriage, Rokeya benefitted from the scholarship of her husband Sakhawat Hossain, who had received his higher education in England. But even before she settled down in Calcutta, before her marriage when she lived in her birthplace Rangpur, Rokeya read European books, mainly through the influence of her elder brothers – Abul Asad Ibrahim Saber and Khalilur Rahman Abu Jaigam Saber – who studied in Calcutta. They were supportive of her informal learning and brought books for her to read. Ibrahim Saber took personal charge of teaching Rokeya at home and in secret so that family members were not aware of her education. Shamsun Nahar Mahmud ([1935] 1996) cites an incident when Ibrahim held a big, illustrated English book before Rokeya and said: "Little sister, if you can learn this language, all the doors to the treasures of the world would be open for you (11)".[3] As the feudalistic, zamindari district Rangpur was connected with Calcutta, 300 miles away, through the rail network as early as 1879, it was not detached from the Calcutta-centred British culture of that time: books and other carriers of civilization came from Calcutta by rail.

In a separate, earlier development, in order to make sure that "the native population would be keen to follow an 'English way of life', at least enough to be good Company servants" (Eaglestone 2009, 11), the colonizers introduced English literature at tertiary level in India in 1835 with the English Education Act. Viswanathan ([1987], 2006) regards this colonial move as "a strategy of containment" that "raises a host of questions about the interrelations of culture, state, and civil society and the modes of assertion of authority within that network of relations" (380). Thus, despite its hegemonic purposes, this colonial strategy opened up a space for Indians to become familiar with English texts. Furthermore, during the colonial period, different publishing firms such as Macmillan and Kegan Paul expanded their business to India and distributed reading materials in the colony (Joshi 2002, 107).

In the face of all impediments, Rokeya made the best use of all available avenues open to her to learn English and to understand the people and culture of Europe. Her knowledge of English was such that she was able to compose impressive literary works such as *Sultana's Dream*. Having described the various ways through which Rokeya came to know English and European people and culture in general, I will discuss in the following section how this knowledge was reflected in her writing.

Europe in Rokeya's work

References to Europe, especially to British writers and colonial incursions into India, are frequent in Rokeya's works. *Gyanphal* is an allegorical story that recounts the process of the British colonial conquest of India, the imperial plunder and transfer of enormous wealth from India to Britain. Bewitched by the arrival of the English colonizers and the glittering progress of England, the Indian people lost their sense of self as well as their freedom. They experienced the loss of their former status and identity and many of them suffered from extreme impoverishment and systematic racial discrimination. In Rokeya's story, Kanakdeep (the Isle of Gold) stands for India, and Poristhan (the Land of Witches) for England.

Rokeya's interactions with European women who question Muslim customs are mentioned in her non-fiction writing. For example, she comments: "Sometimes European sisters say to me, 'Why don't you break off purdah?'" (Hossain [1973] 2006, 43). Elsewhere she notes: "Respected Sister Mrs Lindsey asked me to tell her about the problems of education for Muslim girls" (226). Rokeya's use of the Bangla term *bhogini/gon* (sister/s), a vernacular expression for a friendly and warm relationship, indicates the extent of her familiarity with Europeans in India and the depth of her friendship with them. Moreover, her introduction of English characters like Robinson, Helen and the Reverend Henry White in *Padmarag* (1924) and Sister Sara in *Sultana's Dream*, and references to English women such as Miss Cohen in her keynote address at the Bengal Women's Educational Conference, Miss Duo in the humorous short story "Prem-Rahaswa", to Miss Momgan in her letter to Mamlukul Fatima, and "English lady graduates" who participated as "lady competitors" in "a rhyme competition" in which Rokeya also took part and came first (Hossain [1973] 2006, 518) – all these point to the widespread presence of European people in Bengal and her interaction with them.

Rokeya also comments on English authors such as Ellen Wood (better known as Mrs Henry Wood [1814–87]) along with Marie Corelli (1855–1924), noting their relevance to the condition of Indian women. In particular, she directs readers' attention to Jonathan Swift's *Gulliver's Travels* (1726) and comments that "in the land of Houyhnhnm horses rule whereas human beings (Yahoos) are under their yoke" ([1906] 2006, 430), making use of his literary caricatures and satire on human pretentions and vices, tyranny and the social and political corruption that gripped eighteenth-century England to point to the gender inequalities prevalent in her society. In *Sultana's Dream*, the heroine Sultana makes a voyage to a utopian setting, in allegorical travels similar to those in Swift's novel.

Rokeya's numerous allusions to English literary works and society, and to the plight of women in their sociocultural setting, show the relevance of her works to European readers, since conditions for women in both England and Bengal had similar features. European writers were also of considerable relevance to Rokeya and her local readers since they were undoubtedly aware of European intellectual culture. For instance, according to Himani

Bannerji (1997), Mary Wollstonecraft's *A Vindication of the Rights of Woman* (1792) did not seem "other" to the Indian society in which Bannerji as well as Rokeya was brought up. Drawing upon similarities between women's conditions in England and Bengal, Bannerji insightfully states that "the organisation of everyday life as described in the *Rights of Woman* was familiar to" the Indian social milieu of that time (225). Furthermore, she suggests that it carried for Bengal the important message of "education" and "cultivation of reason" (224) in the lives of women. This message of female education finds sustained expression in Rokeya's writing. All the above allusions and references to Europeans and their culture in Rokeya's work are brief and cursory. However, the most important English work that she discusses in detail, and whose relevance to her society she establishes most fully, is Corelli's *The Murder of Delicia.*

Rokeya's Bangla rendering of *The Murder of Delicia*

Rokeya interpretatively translated sections of *The Murder of Delicia* and creatively transformed its message in terms of her own cultural setting in order to locate commonalities in women's plight globally. Although the source text is over 250 pages, Rokeya's text "Delicia Hotya" spans only 20 pages. This is because she summarizes the text, translates parts of it (Hossain [1973] 2006, 117) and comments on the plot in order to establish its relevance to Bengal, as well as to discount the triumphalist colonial narrative of white women's putative liberation in Europe. She translated not only a text, but also a culture. The commonality between Rokeya's and Corelli's feminist philosophy is palpable, as the former completely reaffirms the latter's concerns for women's social conditions. In Rokeya's writings we notice a global appeal and an urge for unity among "women of different religions, ethnicities and nations" in order to "fight against power structures that are oppressive to women" (Barton 1998, 115), and she exhibits transnational feminist concerns and patterns of thought. At the outset of "Delicia Hotya", Rokeya tells readers what perhaps motivated her to present the story to them. As she states: "While reading the book, I wondered at the similarity between our women and Delicia's story and tended to say: How could Marie Corelli come to know the domestic condition of this wretched India!" (Hossain [1973] 2006, 117).

Rokeya argues that patriarchal social structures and institutions in every society are sustained and strengthened by value systems and cultural rules which propagate the assumption of women's marginality. Patriarchal laws and practices in Europe and Bengal have historically deployed arbitrary distinctions between men and women, and reinforced a culture of violence and systemic discrimination against women. Carlyon in *The Murder of Delicia* says to himself, in reference to his wife Delicia: "Anyway, she is my wife, and she can't get rid of me. She has no fault whatever to find with me in the eyes of the law!" (Corelli 1896, 180; Hossain [1973] 2006, 129). Carlyon exploits Delicia as he knows that the law upholds patriarchy – that it is in his favour, and that it will not heed Delicia's gendered afflictions and deprivations. Rokeya quotes and echoes the outburst that Corelli mentions at the end of the novel:

> Not a tear, not a heart throb of one pure woman wronged shall escape the eyes of Eternal Justice, or fail to bring punishment upon the wrong-doer! This we may believe, – this we MUST believe, – else God Himself would be a demon and the world His Hell! (Corelli 1896, 225; Hossain [1973] 2006, 136)

Rokeya puts forward this revealing question: "How is the life of English women?" People in India may presume that women in Europe are "free, exceptionally talented, equal to men, honoured in society and what not" (117), but as readers peep into the home of Delicia and Carlyon, she informs them that "everything is hollow! […]. In London, the site of civilization and liberty, hundreds of Delicia murder stories are being staged. Alas! Women are defenseless everywhere in the world!" (117). On another occasion, she says, "Men in England used to ridicule brilliant women as 'bluestocking[s]'" (205), revealing her knowledge of an 18th-century term for women's intellectual attainments and conversational wit, and underlining her extensive knowledge of the woman question in England and in Europe in general. Contrary to the outward, dazzling picture of European society, she hints at gender oppression continuing unabated and beyond mere economic quantification, as part of her overview of women's sufferings as a global phenomenon, rather than peculiar to Indian society alone.

Recounting the emotional afflictions of Delicia, who is trapped in matrimonial alliance with an English man, Rokeya concludes that the sufferings of women in Bengal, as in England, are rooted in social, behavioural and cultural systems. English society may seem superficially impressive and gender-egalitarian, but she asks the reader to look at the heart of the woman trapped in the house of Carlyon and assess the extent of her happiness. Given that, despite differences in changing modes of discrimination against women, the causes of their suffering are embedded in the overall social structures and cultural contexts of Europe and India. Hence, Rokeya suggests, there is no good reason to idolize and exaggerate the seemingly advanced standing of women in Europe.

Importantly, Rokeya portrays a symbolic, Indian counterpart to Delicia, through whom she depicts an equally grim picture of the predicament of women as marginalized and discriminated against. The name given to Delicia's Indian "representative" character is Mazluma, derived from an Arabic word meaning "an oppressed woman". Rokeya depicts parallel features of oppression between Delicia and Mazluma, in order to locate common oppressive practices of subjugating women. She also exposes the social construction of gender and women's gendered sufferings in both societies through the representation of cross-cultural characters in her novel *Padmarag* which, alongside the agonies of Indian women like Zaynab and Saudamini, represents the woes and torments of European womanhood in the character of Helen, a victim of "the cruel law of England" (Hossain [1973] 2006, 312). Rokeya also differentiates the condition of women in England from those of Muslim Bengal, finding a strong sense of determination, self-confidence and agency in Corelli's Delicia, which she urges the women of Bengal to emulate. Addressing Carlyon with a pistol in her hand, the spirited Delicia admonishes him:

> "I swear to you that if you come closer to me by one step, or presume to offer me such an insult as your caress would be to me now, I will kill you" (Corelli 1896, 206; Hossain [1973] 2006, 118).

In contrast to the Englishwoman's firm resolve, Rokeya regrets that an Indian woman, in such a situation, would characteristically stoop over the feet of her husband and cry and apologize in a pathetic, rueful tone.

Rokeya also suggests that Delicia's predicament is more intolerable and less acceptable than Mazluma's, commenting on Corelli's depiction of the caring and devoted Delicia as a woman of talents and wealth who gives her hard-earnings from her pen to her spendthrift husband Carlyon who squanders this on gambling and dissolute women: "In this respect

Delicia's condition is more pitiable than that of Mazluma. Wherefore English society claims to be civilized! Is it called civilization? Is it called chivalry?" (Hossain [1973] 2006, 124). She endorses Corelli's contention: "If truth, fidelity and devotion are virtues, then dogs are superior to men; if selfishness, cunning and hypocrisy are virtues, then men are certainly superior to dogs!" (1896, 224–225; Hossain [1973] 2006, 136), confirmed by the fact that Delicia's lapdog Spartan remains faithful and mourns her death profusely, unlike Carlyon who does not. Rokeya even shows, through a conversation between Carlyon and Delicia, that the unproductive domestic enclosure of women causing a sense of alienation was not just peculiar to Indian women, but also prevailed in England. To Carlyon's assertion, "To me the ancient time was good", Delicia replies:

> Maybe? When men used to relegate women to the four walls of the house, in the same way as four-footed animals are fettered and their movement, restricted; they used to give women that much food that they deemed just enough for them to survive; if women were disobedient they used to beat them up? (Hossain [1973] 2006, 121)

In these ways her use of Corelli's text functions as a pretext for critiquing patriarchal manipulations and power structures both in England and Muslim Bengal. Domestic incarceration of women featured not only in the social landscape of Muslim Bengal or India. Interestingly, Carlyon's masculine perception of women – as ideally humble, gentle, absolutely obedient to their husbands, with limited mobility – is identical to the traditional Indian notion of womanhood. He regards his views (that female empowerment would lead to disobedience and insubordination, and that any material endowment should be spent on their husbands) as reflecting a law of nature: that women have been created to serve the interests of men (Corelli 1896, 210; Hossain [1973] 2006, 134).

By sharing the story of Delicia and Carlyon with her readers, Rokeya suggests that men in both India and Europe largely maintain the same perception of gender roles and that the male tendency to police women's movements in order to confine them to the home and deny them their educational and economic rights crosses geographical, religious and cultural boundaries. Interestingly, the character of Jafar in her short play *Shourajagot* (Hossain [1973] 2006) invokes these stereotypical beliefs about femininity, women and their roles in society, so pointing to a convergence of east and west in respect of gender ideology and relationships. Gowhar, acting as Rokeya's spokesperson, heatedly debates with Jafar, representing traditional Bengal society, over women's roles and gender differences. Jafar's views about women closely resemble those of Carlyon, namely that: "Women should not traverse the limitations set by the solar-system-like-society" and that "there is no such limit for men, hence there is no question of transgression on their part" (Hossain [1973] 2006, 98). What is more, he believes that "women should not be given any liberty" (99).

Conclusion

Despite its oppressive and exploitative character, British colonial incursion into India created "a geography of intercultural encounters in contact zones shaped by the historical conditions of modernity, colonialism, and postcolonialism [which facilitated] forms of biological, linguistic, and cultural hybridity, particularly among colonial rulers and indigenous elites" (Friedman 2005, 245–247). As the daughter of a local zamindar and wife of a civil servant, Rokeya belonged to a colonized elite class that enjoyed wealth, education and social standing. Despite her limited enjoyment of these privileges as a woman, she made use of the cultural hybridity of the colonial contact zone, by engaging with Europeans living in British India, and indirectly benefitting from a western-style education: she learned English, read English texts available in colonial Muslim Bengal and creatively represented her perception of Europe and its culture through her writing.

Although her literary career coincided with the height of the anti-colonial Swadeshi movement, the benefits she reaped from the east–west encounter are evident in the perspectives and viewpoints in her work that supersede its colonial milieu. Her modest contestations of colonial hegemony and imperialist domination share Gandhi's understanding of the Swadeshi spirit. Gandhi states: "A true votary of Swadeshi will never harbor ill-will towards the foreigner: he will not be actuated by antagonism towards anybody on earth" (quoted in Giri 2014, 206). To a great extent, Rokeya lived up to this ideal. She devoted herself to literary, educational and political activism at a time when there was animosity in the imperial contact zone of India on two main fronts: between the colonial administration and the nationalists, and between Hindus and Muslims as communal tensions between these two major religious groups in British India "soared largely because of the colonial tactic of 'divide and rule'" (Hasan 2015). Moreover, on a personal level, Rokeya received taunting remarks from the opponents of female education and women's empowerment in her society. However, she rose above all these layers of conflict and tensions (as well as those motivated by personal grievances) and crossed the barriers of racial and communal differences. Even in her campaigns against colonial rule and criticism of discrimination against Muslims, she did not commit any breaches of manners and good taste.

On the linguistic level, during Rokeya's time, Muslims were largely reluctant to learn English. Rokeya maintained no such reservations about the language; she rather promoted the learning of English among Muslims and "mastered" the language herself. Proof of her intercultural position, and command of English, is that her masterpiece *Sultana's Dream*, originally written in English, was translated into Bangla upon requests from readers who wished to read it in the vernacular. This wonderful feminist utopian novella is now taught in western universities. Rokeya's creative practice in English goes against the grain of an anti-western ideology that emphasizes "attitudinal resistance of Muslims towards English and the supposed conflict between English and Islam" (Mohd-Asraf 2005, 103). Muslims in India lost political control to British colonizers, and a supposedly Muslim language (Persian) was replaced by English. In such a cultural context, "Muslims refused to learn English and boycotted Western educational institutions for over half a century" (Ahmed 1982, 262). Moreover, the language was "associated with conquest and colonialism" and "seen as inherently inhospitable to Islam" (Malak 2005, 2). Rokeya not only refused to follow any such linguistic parochialism, but also critiqued her Muslim community for such an imprudent stance (Hossain [1973] 2006, 491).

It was in this spirit of openness and transcending borders that Rokeya learnt the English language, interacted with the colonizers and informed her readers about Corelli and her novel. She imagined Europe and depicted the condition of women of Muslim Bengal and those from England in order to identify shared experiences of womanhood globally and to dispel the widely held perception that, unlike women in Bengal, English women were fully empowered. Rokeya argues that women in both societies are subjugated by patriarchal power, an insight which points to her broader, transnational feminist concerns beyond the borders of Bengal.

Notes

1. In this article I refer to her as "Rokeya" but, for the sake of consistency with conventional academic practices, in citations and bibliographic references list her name under "Hossain".
2. In this article, Europe/European and England/English are used interchangeably. Although India was colonized by the British, in Rokeya's society they were referred to generically as Europeans.
3. English translations of all Bangla source texts are my own, unless otherwise stated.

Acknowledgements

An earlier version of this article was presented at *Imaginary Europes* (University of Portsmouth, UK on 13 September 2012). The author gratefully acknowledges the comments he received from the participants of the conference.

Funding

This work was supported by the Research Management Centre, International Islamic University Malaysia [EDW A13-005-1432].

References

Ahmed, Munir D. 1982. "Pakistan: The Dream of an Islamic State." In *Religion and Societies: Asia and the Middle East*, edited by Carlo Caldarola, 261–288. Berlin: Mouton.

Aiyar, Chetpat Pattabhirama Ramaswami. 1963. *Annie Besant*. Delhi: Ministry of Information and Broadcasting, Government of India.

Amin, Sonia Nishat. 1996. *The World of Muslim Women in Colonial Bengal, 1876–1939*. Leiden: Brill.

Bannerji, Himani. 1997. "Mary Wollstonecraft, Feminism and Humanism: A Spectrum of Reading." In *Mary Wollstonecraft and 200 Years of Feminisms*, edited by Eileen J. Yeo, 222–242. London: Rivers Oram Press.

Barton, Mukti. 1998. "Rokeya Sakhawat Hossain and the Bengali Muslim Women's Movement." *Dialogue and Alliance* 12 (1): 105–116.

Botting, Eileen Hunt. 2006. *Family Feuds: Wollstonecraft, Burke, and Rousseau on the Transformation of the Family*. New York: State University of New York Press.

Brass, Paul R. 2000. "Elite Groups, Symbol Manipulation and Ethnic Identity among the Muslims of South Asia." In *Nationalism: Critical Concepts in Political Science*. vol. 3, edited by John Hutchinson and Anthony D. Smith, 879–911. London: Routledge.

Burton, Antoinette M. 1994. *Burdens of History: British Feminists, Indian Women, and Imperial Culture, 1865–1915*. Chapel Hill, NC: University of North Carolina Press.

Corelli, Marie. 1896. *The Murder of Delicia*. London: Constable & Company.

Deshpande, Arvind M., Paranjpe Shrikant, Dixit Raja, and C. R. Das. 1997. *Western India: History, Society, and Culture*. Maharashtra: Itihas Shikshak Mahamanda.

Dinakarlal, J. 2014. "Christian Higher Education in India: The Road We Tread." In *Christian Higher Education: A Global Reconnaissance*, edited by Joel Carpenter, Perry L. Glanzer and Nicholas S. Lantinga, 111–133. Cambridge: Wm. B. Eerdmans.

Eaglestone, Robert. 2009. *Doing English: A Guide for Literature Students*. London: Routledge.

Friedman, Susan Stanford. 2005. "Paranoia, Pollution, and Sexuality: Affiliations between E. M. Forster's *a Passage to India* and Arundhati Roy's *the God of Small Things*." In *Geomodernisms: "Race,"Modernism, Modernity*, edited by Laura Doyle and Laura A. Winkiel, 245–261. Bloomington, IN: Indiana University Press.

Giri, Ananta Kumar. 2014. *Knowledge and Human Liberation: Towards Planetary Realizations*. New York: Anthem Press.

Hasan, Md Mahmudul. 2013. "Commemorating Rokeya Sakhawat Hossain and Contextualising Her Work in South Asian Muslim Feminism." *Asiatic* 7 (2): 39–59.

Hasan, Md Mahmudul. 2015. "Rokeya's Tolerance and Magnanimity." *Daily Star* (Dhaka) December 9. http://www.thedailystar.net/country/opinion-rokeyas-tolerance-and-magnanimity-184591

Hossain, Rokeya Sakhawat. [1973] 2006. *Rokeya Rachanabali*. edited by Abdul Quadir. Dhaka: Bangla Academy.

Hunter, William Wilson. 1871. *Indian Mussalmans*. London: Williams and Norgate.

Inden, Ronald. 1990. *Imagining India*. Oxford: Blackwell.

Joshi, Priyo. 2002. *In Another Country: Colonialism, Culture, and the English Novel in India*. New York: Columbia University Press.

Lambert-Hurley, Siobhan. 2007a. *Muslim Women, Reform and Princely Patronage: Nawab Sultan Jahan Begam of Bhopal*. Oxford: Routledge.

Lambert-Hurley, Siobhan. 2007b. *A Princess's Pilgrimage: Nawab Sikandar Begum's "a Pilgrimage to Mecca"*. Markfield: Kube Publishing.

Lambert-Hurley, Siobhan, and Sunil Sharma. 2010. *Atiya's Journeys: A Muslim Woman from Colonial Bombay to Edwardian Britain*. New Delhi: Oxford University Press.

Mahmud, Shamsun Nahar. [1935] 1996. *Rokeya Jibani*. 2nd ed. Calcutta: Noya Udwog.

Malak, Amin. 2005. *Muslim Narratives and the Discourse of English*. New York: State University of New York Press.

Mann, Michael. 2004. "Dealing with Oriental Despotism: British Jurisdiction in Bengal, 1772-93." In *Colonialism as Civilising Mission: Cultural Ideology in British India*, edited by Harald Fischer-Tiné and Michael Mann, 29–48. London: Anthem Press.

Mill, John Stuart. 1869. *The Subjection of Women*. London: Longmans, Green, Reader and Dyer.

Mohd-Asraf, Ratnawati. 2005. "English and Islam: A Clash of Civilizations?" *Journal of Language, Identity & Education* 4 (2): 103–118.

Murshid, Ghulam. 1983. *Reluctant Debutante: Response of Bengali Women to Modernization, 1849–1905*. Rajshahi: Sahitya Samsad.

Nayar, Pramod K. 2008. *Postcolonial Literature: An Introduction*. Delhi: Pearson-Longman.

Roy, Parama. 1998. *Indian Traffic: Identities in Question in Colonial and Postcolonial India*. Berkeley, CA: University of California Press.

Sarkar, Mahua. 2008. *Visible Histories, Disappearing Women: Producing Muslim Womanhood in Late Colonial Bengal*. Durham, NC: Duke University Press.

Viswanathan, Gauri. [1987] 2006. "The Beginnings of English Literary Study in British India." In *The Post-Colonial Studies Reader*, edited by Bill Ashcroft, Gareth Griffiths, and Helen Tiffin, 376–380. London: Routledge.

Panchayat and colonialism in Humayun Kabir's *Men and Rivers*

Md. Mahmudul Hasan

ABSTRACT

Bengali peasants, as portrayed in Humayun Kabir's 1945 novel *Men and Rivers*, have admirable notions of morality and justice, epitomized by the indigenous panchayat (village council/court) system. Written against the backdrop of peasant movements and anti-colonial struggles in Bengal, the novel implicitly provides an economic and cultural critique of British rule in the region. This article situates the text in colonial Bengal and the peasant revolutions of the 1930s. Referring to Frantz Fanon's valorization of the peasants, it discusses Kabir's depiction in *Men and Rivers* of the simplicity, integrity, and altruism of the peasantry as opposed to the sleaze and hypocrisy of colonialism and colonial modernity. It juxtaposes panchayat and colonialism to show the native peasants' egalitarian potential and the encroaching colonizers' exploitative motives, looks at Kabir's celebration of rural traditions, and compares the South Asian panchayat system to its African counterparts – *djemaas* in northern, and *kgotla* in southern, Africa.

Introduction: The backdrop of colonial Bengal

In 1947, upon the British withdrawal from the region, the Indian subcontinent was partitioned on religious lines. Hindus and Sikhs internally migrated to Hindu-majority India, and Muslims to Muslim-majority Pakistan. Though a Muslim and born in Muslim-majority East Bengal (later East Pakistan and now Bangladesh), in 1947, the politician, poet, essayist, and novelist Humayun Kabir (1906–69) chose India as his home. However, since he was born and raised in what is now Bangladesh, he is regarded as a Bangladeshi writer for reasons of provenance from the spatial (not temporal) boundary of the country.

Among Bangladeshi novels in English, Kabir's (1945) *Men and Rivers* stands out for dedicating its entire plot to exploring a rural society and pitting it against colonial incursions, modernity, and exploitation. Given the spatial and temporal setting of the novel, its colonial undertones cannot be ignored. It was published at the height of the anti-colonial movement and only two years before India's independence from Britain in 1947. Most importantly, the Swadeshi (native) movement of the early 20th century, that called for a boycott of foreign products in favour of domestic ones and supported independence from colonialism, originated from Kabir's Bengal but later spread to other parts of British India, broadening the base of anti-colonial struggle. Given Kabir's lifelong political consciousness and activism, it is inconceivable that he would remain isolated from *la condition humaine* when writing *Men and Rivers*. Textual evidence, which I discuss below, suggests that its setting is British colonial Bengal.

First, in the story, once the character Malek is orphaned early on after losing his father (Nazu Mia) and grandmother (Ayesha), the male farmhand Basir and female domestic helps Kulsum and Gulabi become Malek's surrogate guardians. As Basir is unable to collect rent on behalf of Malek from the tenants of sandbank lands that the latter has inherited from his father, the three guardians contemplate what to do with those properties. They dismiss the idea of selling them because the sale proceeds (money) in the house may attract the attention of robbers, put their lives in danger, and make Malek a pauper. Nor can they "deposit it with the *Mahajan* [moneylender], for then [they will] never see it again" (Kabir 1945, 78). Notably, the *mahajan* culture was widespread in British colonial Bengal. As Novak (1993) states, "under the British most landowners and moneylenders, or mahajans, were Hindus who kept their peasant tenants in a state of serfdom unmatched by any civilized society in this century" (78).

In Bengal, there were strong peasant movements against the (economic) oppression on the part of landlords and moneylenders – the zamindars and *mahajans* – most of whom were Hindu (Aiyar 2008, 1218; Ahmed 1971, 4), and preyed upon "the common people, the Muslim majority and the Hindu minority" (Novak 1993, 149). The majority Muslim peasants were organized mainly under the leadership of A.K. Fazlul Huq (1873–1962) who along with other Muslim leaders formed the Praja (tenant) Party (later renamed Krishak Praja [peasant-tenant] Party) that was active in the 1930s. At that time, Kabir was one of its prominent members; he was elected on its ticket to the Bengal Legislative Assembly in 1937 elections and became the vice president of its parliamentary group, while Huq became the chief minister of united Bengal. In parts of East Bengal and Assam, in the eventful 1930s, Maulana Abdul Hamid Khan Bhashani (1880–1976) became popular for organizing a peasant social movement (Rashiduzzaman 1970, 575). Political consciousness among the peasants at that time was so strong that, even though prominent Muslim League politicians belonged to the upper class, "Bengal's Independent Muslim League represented not the ashraf [elite] but workers and peasants" (Novak 1993, 153). While writing *Men and Rivers*, Kabir's mind was understandably alive to these peasant movements. In his later work he celebrates "peasants, workers and other labouring classes" and argues that "these humbler vocations are as important for the survival of society as the work of those who give themselves superior airs" (Kabir 1968, 103), as he seeks to bring them within the purview of literature. The fact that most Bengali peasants were Muslim explains Kabir's depiction of an all-Muslim society in *Men and Rivers*.

Second, after Malek is taken hostage by a group of pirates later in the story, Mang Po, their sardar (chief), encourages him to join the band of robbers. Upon his refusal to do so, Mang Po says: "We are not robbers but rovers of the sea. We recognize no law but our own". But Malek replies: "Then you see, *Sardar*, how different are our two points of view. I have been taught to obey the King's law and submit" (Kabir 1945, 157). In all likelihood, through Malek's statement, the novelist is referring to a post-Victorian, early-20th-century British monarch and his colonial rule in Bengal. Even though Mang Po has a *harmad* (Portuguese sea pirate) named Donpedo (a variant of Don Pedo) in his band, this should not suggest a shift in the temporal setting of the novel to an earlier period – the 15th and 16th centuries – when Mogh Portuguese piracy was an endemic menace, especially in the coastal areas adjacent to the Bay of Bengal. The fact that there is only one *harmad* in Mang Po's band indicates the dwindling Portuguese population in the region. Portuguese descendants are still present in Bengal (Choudhury 2002) and their influence was palpable during the British colonial period, since Robert Clive (1725–74), the first British Governor of the Bengal Presidency, used the Portuguese language to communicate "with the native troops under his command" (Steel 2015). At odds with British colonial interests, the "Portuguese may well have taken to a level of piracy, especially in alliance with the Arakanese" (Steel 2015) known as Moghs – an appellation the Europeans gave to the natives of Arakan (now Rakhine state in Myanmar).

Third, the signboard that the Hakim (doctor) in *Men and Rivers* places on top of his shop in the village market of Dhuldi and which gives him a special status among the villagers also suggests that the setting of the novel is British colonial Bengal. In the novel, the peasants are ignorant of the letters of the signboard – presumably written in English. In most British colonies, "[s]hop sign-boards which incorporated foreign language, in this case English, were perceived as prestigious" (Salleh and Abdullah 2017, 43). Although the existence of signboards in the subcontinent goes back millennia (Sharma 2004), organized shops and commercial signboards were a British introduction. In Britain, "[b]y the seventeenth century, English laws required that every craftsman or tradesman exhibit a sign that presented the products and services provided" (Mircea 2019). Conversely, in pre-colonial Bengal, a shop was known by its owner and their profession; but colonialism brought "urban anonymity" and signboards became important to declare the existence of the trader and to describe their trade (Syed Manzoorul Islam, personal communication, May 8, 2022).

Even though in *Men and Rivers* Kabir does not make explicit reference to colonial rule, the above discussion shows that the novel is set in British colonial Bengal. However, despite pervasive colonial influences, the everyday life of the peasants portrayed in the text continues to be shaped by local norms and customs and governed by the panchayat (village council/court) system. This emphasis seems to anticipate Frantz Fanon's (1963) incisive assertion that, as opposed to the colonized city-dwellers, it is the peasantry that represents the true anti-colonialist element of a nation: "in colonial countries only the peasantry is revolutionary. It has nothing to lose and everything to gain" (23). Deeply rooted in a vision of the North African peasantry, Fanon's dialectic of decolonization rejects elitism and urban centralism and invokes a structural opposition to colonialism, which is the subject of this article.

Kabir seeks to restore and recapture the humanity and dignity of the peasant victims of colonialism who are situated "below" the dominant groups in colonized societies. Even though there is no evidence to suggest that Kabir and Fanon engaged with each other's texts, Sameer Pandya (2001) extensively establishes the relevance of Fanon's ideas to late British India. In *The Wretched of the Earth* (Fanon 1963), published nearly two decades after *Men and Rivers*, Fanon seems to confirm Kabir's affirmative and laudatory notion of the peasantry. However, while Fanon emphasizes "the revolutionary potential of the peasants" (Pandya 2001, 23) and espouses violent anti-colonial struggles, in *Men and Rivers* Kabir's anti-colonial message is non-violent, reflective, and sublime. Kabir's tactical, pacifist philosophy can be attributed to Mahatma Gandhi's "programme of non-violent non-cooperation", as Kabir regards "the concept of non-violent method" as a distinctive characteristic of the Indian Revolution, adding: "[a]cceptance of non-violence and persuasion has paid even greater dividends within the country. The whole Princely order has become a thing of the past, and yet not one Prince was killed" (Kabir 1960, 3, 21–22).

Given this theoretical foundation, the present article looks at politico-economic and cultural relations in *Men and Rivers*, especially through the prism of the postcolonial critique of imperial power, mounted a decade later by Frantz Fanon. It discusses characters in the story who are local beneficiaries of colonialism. Kwame Anthony Appiah (1992) calls such people "a comprador intelligentsia" that comprises "a relatively small, Western-style, Western-trained, group of writers and thinkers, who mediate the trade in cultural commodities of world capitalism at the periphery" (149). In the novel, Kabir dissects the characters of this colonized minority – who are not necessarily writers but have colonial complicity/sophistication – and pits them against their local others. Accordingly, the discussion that follows underscores Kabir's admiration for rural values and the peasant, indigenous way of life which will be contrasted with his veiled denunciation of colonial economic and cultural hegemony represented by two comprador natives – the Dewan (an agent of colonial economic oppression) and the Hakim (an embodiment of colonial cultural influence). Such privileged natives, in the words of Fanon, "by their activities and by their complicity with the occupier have dishonored their country" (1963, 132). Though not explicitly taken up in *Men and Rivers*, as discussed above, colonialism, with its economic and cultural relations, is pertinent to the story as a whole and informs its political-historical context.

Mainstreaming the peasants

As regards the subject matter of *Men and Rivers*, Kabir, like his contemporary (in time and place) Jasimuddin (1903–76), known as *pallikobi* (rural/folkloric poet), "remained identified with the peasantry among whom he had been born", to use Syed Sajjad Husain's ([1994] 2022, 187) words. Even though Kabir hailed from an upper-class family and the British gave his father the honorary title of Khan Bahadur, both his involvement in Huq's Praja Party and his writing point to his concern for and affiliation with the peasants. This attachment to his society of origin corresponds to his regard for what he himself calls, in his *The Bengali Novel*, "stark realism and first-hand knowledge of the hardship and privations of rural life" (Kabir 1968, 115).

Although politically Kabir was not drawn to the left,[1] in his depiction of rural life and its problems he can be regarded as belonging to a "new class of writers who were influenced by Marx [and] chose as their heroes and heroines men and women from what are usually regarded as the lower classes" (Kabir 1968, 103). Kabir's concept of the "lower classes" is comparable to Fanon's notion of the "peasantry" as a group within the colonized society that is "systematically left out of most of the nationalist parties' propaganda" (Fanon 1963, 23). While Fanon is concerned with the French–Algerian colonial (political) context, Kabir's focus is on colonial Bengal's cultural one. In both milieus, poor agricultural labourers and rural marginalized peasants are overlooked – a neglect that Kabir seeks to repair in order to promote an egalitarian literary culture.

In colonial and postcolonial South Asia, the political and intellectual elites in urban centres have mainly used English for communication and intellectual work. This explains the fact that most Bangladeshi anglophone writers are trained in English literature, which carries with it prestige and "the specific weight of an entire civilization" (Amoko 2001, 35) in postcolonial settings. In their writings, they often deal with issues far removed from those that preoccupy the peasant and farming class. Kabir is at variance with such literary accounts of a society like Bengal, pointing out that "[t]he peasants constitute over sixty per cent of the total population and yet most Bengali novels [...] deal with the life of the middle and lower middle class in urbanized areas" (1968, 119–120). Accordingly, Kabir describes the life of the peasantry and places English words in the mouths of people who are generally not accustomed to using the language, and thus mainstreams them into linguistic and literary discourse and puts them on a level with the educated *bhadralok* (the elites of colonial Bengal).

In *Men and Rivers*, the village Rahimpur,[2] the *hat* (village market) at Dhuldi, and the coastal island of Byanchar – all rural – are three prominent settings. Rahimpur and Dhuldi are not far from Kabir's birthplace Komarpur in Faridpur district, while Byanchar is at the mouth of the Bay of Bengal "near the confluence of the Padma with the sea" (Kabir 1945, 122). Through Rahimpur, Kabir depicts a slice of rural Faridpur that has its own organized society and rule of law but exists only a stone's throw away from Dhuldi, where colonialism has a marked impact and creates conditions for exploitation.[3] Being an island newly formed by sedimentation and far away from colonial centres, Byanchar is not influenced or eroded by colonialism in any shape or form (for a detailed discussion of Byanchar, see Hasan 2022). Conversely, "renowned for its ancient history and colonial architecture",[4] Faridpur was a crucible of colonial encounter and "one of the main terminals connecting Calcutta with Goalanda.[5] It was also a vital river port where many ships departed for Assam and Burma in the [colonial] period" (Turza 2021, 243–244). What is more, "[i]n 1895 the A[s]sam–Bengal rail-line started to expand" to the Goalanda–Calcutta one which stretched to Faridpur (Turza 2021, 245). All these communication networks facilitated colonial penetration in the area.

Accordingly, in *Men and Rivers*, Dhuldi is portrayed as an outpost of colonialism that impacts the life of the peasantry in the surrounding areas, as the "*hat* at Dhuldi was the centre of village life for miles around" (Kabir 1945, 12). The colonial culture and apparatus of power that extended to Dhuldi is shown as exploiting the people of Rahimpur economically without disrupting the village's traditional rule of law and conventional concepts of individual dignity, rights, and social justice. Its rule of law rests on the strong foundation of the panchayat system, which will be outlined in the following section.

The panchayat principle of justice

Associated with the Sanskrit word *pancha* (five), the term "panchayat" refers to an assembly/group of five influential elders who are chosen by community consensus to intervene in and conduct social affairs. However, the number is not necessarily constant, as the panchayat "may include more than five elders, who authoritatively direct the villagers and help to resolve their disputes" (Vincentnathan 2001, 30). The smallest unit of governance of informal nature in rural South Asia, the panchayat takes the principal role in disciplining members of the community and adjudicates on antisocial behaviour, social crimes, marital discord, economic misconduct, and individual and collective issues of various kinds within agreed upon parameters. Interestingly, there are comparable "traditional legislative fora [such] as the *djemaas* or the village assembly" in northern Africa and "*kgotla* in Botswana" (Lazarus 1993, 76). As Kabir commends the South Asian panchayat system, so does Fanon in describing these African village gatherings or informal courts of law where people discuss community and legal issues: "Whether in the *djemaas* of northern Africa or in the meetings of western Africa, tradition demands that the quarrels which occur in a village should be settled in public" (Fanon 1963, 48). Like *djemaa* and *kgotla* (open-air court) meetings, traditionally, the panchayat sessions are held in an open public space or in the yard of an influential villager, even though in *Men and Rivers* such discussions take place inside the masjid and generally after the villagers have performed ritual prayers. The depiction of this important commonality between the subcontinental and African traditions suggests that there is much to celebrate in the pre-colonial past of most non-western societies.

Dating back to India's pre-Mughal times and often regarded as a "Hindu form of arbitration" (Jaffe 2014, 148), the panchayat system is common among all religious groups in South Asia. With the arrival of Islam, the Mughal rulers introduced a central court administration without eliminating "the village justice systems" or panchayats (Iyer and Hoben 2018, 221). Initially, during the colonial period, the panchayat system had been undermined, as the British introduced English law and emphasized codified religious texts. However, as the consultative nature of the panchayat system makes it somewhat "analogous to the English jury", the British changed their approach to it over time and accepted it as "a tribunal [... or] a board of arbitration" that "provided an inexpensive and speedy forum for alternative dispute resolution" (Jaffe 2014, 131–132). Hence, the representation of this pre-colonial panchayat system in the novel does not negate the colonial character of its setting and it presents an alternative model of rule, one opposed to European imperialism.

Men and Rivers depicts the panchayat system in Rahimpur as determining the nature of village life and exercising social and judicial control over the village's members. The peasants in Rahimpur have an organized life of their own characterized by group fellowship and discipline. In all aspects of social and community life, the panchayat is held in high esteem. Even though the panchayat is a village council, in the novel the head of the panchayat is seen as its embodiment and is referred to as the panchayat. The panchayat Nazu Mia (like his successor Asgar Mia) commands unquestioned respect among the people, as Rahimpur's way of life lies outside the class-based confines of colonial respectability that has encroached upon Dhuldi. Although in the traditional leadership model, the chief panchayat is at the centre of power, *matabbars* (village influentials) act as his assistants and hold sway in the villagers' lives. Accordingly, the panchayat system Kabir depicts in the novel is not an autocracy because the chief "can't decide anything entirely on his own. The *matabbars* will meet and discuss, and come to a decision" (Kabir 1945, 78). Moreover, it is founded on a culture of trust, and a trust deficit can result in the loss of position on the part of the panchayat chief (96).

Kabir portrays animosity between Nazu Mia and his rival (in power and social influence), Asgar Mia, and observes that the village contains "robbers and thieves" (Kabir 1945, 90) as well as the wily and rather mischievous young character Sabu.

Nevertheless, truth and justice are the guiding principles of the system of law in effect in Rahimpur. As regards his guardianship of Malek (son of his opponent Nazu Mia), Asgar Mia emphasizes the need to do justice even to an enemy. As the orphan Malek or his guardian Basir cannot manage the former's sandbank lands, through the latter's initiative and a consultative decision-making process, Asgar Mia takes charge of those lands. As the panchayat Asgar Mia is indeed a pillar of equity and justice in society, the *matabbars* also share the same concern for fair play and the welfare of all in the village.

In Rahimpur, bravery and heroism are associated with leadership, social influence, and respect, while deceit and dishonesty are considered morally abhorrent. Conversely, the *hat* at Dhuldi emerges as what Mary Louise Pratt (1992) calls the "contact zone" created by colonial domination and characterized by "conditions of coercion, radical inequality and intractable conflict" (6). As a complex, hybrid space and an imperial contact zone open to multiple influences, Dhuldi has turned into a crucible of colonial interactions and an intricate web of imperialist control and malpractices. While the unnamed character holding the position of the tax collector Dewan (or Diwan) in Dhuldi is an agent of colonial exploitation and venality, the doctor based in the *hat* and referred to as the Hakim in the story is another nameless character who embodies the artificiality and hypocrisy of colonial modernity, as I shall argue in what follows.

Colonial incursions: The Dewan in Dhuldi

Even though Rahimpur society in the story is marginal and detached from colonial attitudes and behaviours, as well as from the corrosive influence of colonial culture, colonialism and its effects have penetrated the neighbouring Dhuldi. During the colonial period in South Asia, such remote places as Dhuldi were permeated by colonial modernity and administrative machinery and visited by its furthest outlying agent, the Dewan who – though often a local – was appointed by, and owed "primary allegiance" to, the British (Varghese 2009, 13). In the novel, the Dewan comes to Dhuldi "at the full moon" every month to collect land taxes and unless the villagers clear their "due" they "lose [their] lands" to him (Kabir 1945, 46). This resonates with the way in which Bengal society was "completely monopolized by the East India Company's colonial state [...] in the late eighteenth and early nineteenth centuries" (Davini 2009, 62) and later by direct colonial rule. People were compelled to transform their mode of life and accept the new colonial reality by handing over taxes and being subjected to resource exploitation.

Historically, in 1579 during the reign of Mughal Emperor Akbar (1542–1605, r. 1556–1605), the "office of Dewan [finance minister] was established to oversee taxation and the management of revenue collection" (Brown 2010, 7). With the introduction of this new office, Mughal officials expanded their trade and commerce. Later, as the British colonizers strengthened their grip on state apparatuses and populations, the last Nawab (provincial governor) of independent Bengal, Siraj-ud-Daulah (1733–57, r. 1756–57) had profound misgivings about their presence and trade activities in the region. His aversion to the East India Company's growing influence cost him his throne and life. The Company official Robert Clive and his mercenaries launched a military expedition against him; the Battle of Plassey was fought, and the Nawab was defeated on June 23,

1757 and executed on July 2, 1757. Subsequently, Clive "acquired for the English Company real control of Bengal, Behar, and Orissa, and finally the [...] office of dewan" (Jones 1920, 606).

The Company's diwani (revenue-collecting powers) in these areas led to its ability to administer and establish full control over financial and military affairs and gradually to the British occupation of India. By virtue of the office of dewan, the British began to expand their diverse influences from Bengal to other regions and consolidate their hold over the entire subcontinent. Throughout British India, the Company appointed European dewans who were assisted by their local counterparts. Soon the entire diwani system became corruption-ridden and "greedy Company agents lost all restraint and began the process of economically plundering Bengal [and] readily assumed the rights of accepting bribes, pocketing tax revenues, and smuggling goods" (Brown 2010, 24). The Company, its officials (including Clive) and the British government all exploited the grant of diwani to pillage the colonized in various ways.

Similarly, in *Men and Rivers*, as opposed to the moral foundation of honesty of the panchayat system in place in Rahimpur, the Dewan establishes a regime of bribery and power abuse in Dhuldi. He comes to Dhuldi every month to extract land revenues from the peasants and impose penalties on those who are unable or unwilling to pay. As Basir is unable to collect rent, in order to keep the Dewan from confiscating Malek's land, Ayesha's ornaments and Gulabi's and Kulsum's trinkets are sold to pay taxes. He makes multiple trips across the Padma to collect rent from the tenants, but every time comes back home empty-handed.

Under the circumstances, Basir informs the clerk of the Dewan about the problem of not getting rent from the tenants; but the clerk replies in a tone of summary dismissal and cold fury: "What have I got to do with your quarrels? I want my revenue in proper time. So long as I get my rent, you may go on fighting like cats for all I care" (Kabir 1945, 76). When Basir seeks to garner sympathy by mentioning that the owner of the land is an orphan (Malek), the clerk suggests that it be transferred to capable hands and indicates that, if given a hefty bribe, he will arrange the transfer of its ownership to Basir. Basir occupies the moral high ground and remains above such a nefarious scheme of grabbing an orphan's property. Thus, as opposed to colonial depravity, Kabir depicts the household of Nazu Mia – that includes Basir, Gulabi, and Kulsum – as a microcosm of a world order that is grounded in uprightness, compassion, and concern for others.

The social order that Nazu Mia was instrumental in constructing, and which is sustained after him by Asgar Mia, is based on good morals and ethical values. At one point, after Nazu Mia's death, Sabu prods Malek to take part in merrymaking, using someone else's boat. When it is clear to Malek that the boat belongs to a person unknown to him and that using it without the owner's permission is unethical, he resists for some time the temptation to enjoy the boat ride with other children, saying: "My father always said that I must not take other men's boats" (Kabir 1945, 67). After persistent urging by Sabu, Malek finally relents and joins the clique to enjoy rough sports in the river. Once Malek is back home, his guardians Basir and Kulsum show displeasure that he has participated in an adventure that involved stealing a boat. While Kulsum's rebuke and reprimand is fiery and expressive, Basir's is intended to stir Malek's conscience, repentance, and sense of honour. He says to Malek:

> You must remember you are Nazu Mia's son. Your father was the most respected man in our land and you must grow up so that you can one day take his place. What would your father say, if he were alive today? (74–75).

Thus, against the backdrop of colonial immorality and in face of the forces of imperial exploitation as found in the rural centre of Dhuldi and exemplified by the character of the Dewan, Kabir depicts in the microcosm of Nazu Mia's household an alternative society where such vices and abuses have no place. While the Dewan in Dhuldi stands as a typical representative of colonial power and an agent of its economic despotism, the Hakim in the village market is quintessentially a specimen of colonial modernity; the following section elaborates on this.

The doctor in Dhuldi

The doctor or the Hakim is one of the few people in Dhuldi who can read and write. Since the narrator regards Nazu Mia as "local" (Kabir 1945, 15) in relation to the doctor, though a colonized subject, the latter is understandably not from this locality and is presumably from an urban background. He belongs to what Fanon calls

> intellectuals, and shopkeepers, all living for the most part in the towns. Their way of thinking is already marked in many points by the comparatively well-to-do class [...]. It is these classes that will [...] change old customs, and that will thus enter into open conflict with the old granite block upon which the nation rests. (1963, 109)

In the context of Kabir's colonial Bengal, a section of society, termed the "comprador" class in postcolonial discourse as discussed before, came into contact with colonial masters, received colonial education, and in some way can be regarded as what Gayatri Spivak would call "native informants" (1988, 284). They are dominant, "know", and have "all of the problems of selfhood" while "the self of the Other is authentic without a problem" (Spivak 1990, 66). In *Men and Rivers*, while Nazu Mia is a colonized Other but with an authentic identity, the Hakim exhibits imitation and mimicry of colonial behaviour, has a self that is compromised, and is a misfit in the local culture.

As previously discussed, the Hakim "had put a sign-board on which his name is displayed in bold letters" (Kabir 1945, 12). This visual medium is in some ways a non-linguistic symbol for the illiterate villagers and designed to give an impression of urban, colonial sophistication. As a mark of (colonial) modernity, education, and civilization in a small, influential subgroup of society, it is set against the traditions and customs of rural life. The structure is important only in conveying a message that the Hakim does not belong to the category of the subaltern classes in the peripheries or their way of life and deserves special treatment because of his education. The text that it displays and the one that is contained in his books are significantly less important than what they symbolize. They confirm his claim to literacy and difference. The disconnect between the Hakim and the peasants also typifies what Fanon calls "the lack of practical links between [the colonized educated gentry] and the mass of the people" (1963, 148). The signboard and what it represents can also be seen as a mark of deception, as explicated below.

The episode that involves a crocodile being caught on Malek's fishing line in the Padma River morphs and is mythologized in different versions at the marketplace at Dhuldi. The ten-year old Malek is miraculously transformed into a legendary hero and his father Nazu Mia also merits extra attention from the crowd. The Hakim seeks to take advantage of the simplicity of rustic life, as he embodies the artificiality and complexity intricately interwoven in the thought and practice of the modern-educated class. Kabir pits an example of the colonial *bhadralok* class – the Hakim – against his material and social base and presents him as detached from it.

While the villagers at the Dhuldi *hat* focus on the crocodile story and dissect its various aspects and episodes, the Hakim eyes the reptile itself. As Nazu Mia revels in the glory of his and Malek's centrality all around the *hat*, the doctor invites him to sit on the *farash* (felted floor covering of wool and/or cotton) at his shop. Like the signboard on top of his shop, the *farash* on the floor is also highly symbolic. Through the *farash*, the Hakim creates a Manichaean division between the elite and the people, between himself and the peasantry. In this dualistic structure, Nazu Mia and the Hakim occupy mutually exclusive positions. Nazu Mia is no ordinary villager; he is the panchayat vested with considerable power and authority in Rahimpur and with the responsibility of administering its affairs. However, the doctor's shop adheres to a different norm of respectability antithetical to that prevailing in Rahimpur. Previously, Nazu Mia was never asked to sit on the *farash*, as he does not meet the value standards that the Hakim has set in his shop. The Hakim participates in "othering" the villagers and maintains a pseudo-colonialist distance from them while at the same time trying to take advantage of their labour and innocence.

After the crocodile incident, the Hakim goes against his (false) etiquette and shows an unusual respect to Nazu Mia by letting him relax on the *farash* and smoke the hookah for a while, while resorting to flattery and other forms of emotional manipulation. Soon it becomes obvious that the Hakim's hospitality towards Nazu Mia is nothing but his cunning art tainted with insincerity and designed to manoeuvre his guest. Finally, the Hakim discloses his intention of obtaining the crocodile's spleen to use as "a specific against rheumatism and gout and also for general debility", and the crocodile's liver to make a special medicine to increase "strength and courage" (Kabir 1945, 15). Upon hearing the Hakim's request for these two organs, Nazu Mia frankly admits his ignorance of such medicinal benefits of the water creature and informs his host that the carcase has already been thrown into the river. Despairing at this revelation, the Hakim shows his real face to Nazu Mia. Now the fact that Nazu Mia has sat on the *farash* seems "presumptuous" to him. As the narrator puts it, "[t]he Hakim felt he would like to snub Nazu Mia and tell him that his place was the uncovered platform used by rustics and plebians" (Kabir 1945, 15) – this despite the fact that Nazu Mia has not taken a seat on the *farash* uninvited.

The Hakim seeks to demean Nazu Mia by referring to his arch-rival Asgar Mia in leadership roles, saying: "Well, if you have thrown away the carcase […] I however hope to get the spleen and liver from Asgar Mia" (Kabir 1945, 15). The reference to Asgar Mia is suggestive and is meant to trigger a psychological tension between the two local competitors and contribute to their ongoing rivalry and race for public prestige and domination. Nazu Mia retorts with a sneer that "[i]f Asgar has promised you a crocodile, you might begin to prepare your specific" (15–16). This sweet-and-sour remark shows Nazu Mia's ability to gain an edge over the Hakim in conversational skills. The Hakim's attempt to intensify the bitterness between these two erstwhile friends – now adversaries – can also be interpreted as an outsider's interference in local matters for nefarious interests. This somehow resonates with the Dewan's ploy to create a rift between

Malek and Basir by instigating the latter to grab the former's land. All of this is perhaps a reflection of the broader colonial tactics of divide and rule and Kabir's skilful application of this political strategy at a micro level.

Having failed to belittle Nazu Mia's sense of self-worth and self-esteem, the Hakim stoops lower and points to Nazu Mia's physical uncouthness and apparent lack of taste and sophistication. He turns his eyes to Nazu Mia's bare feet and considers them uncared for, dirty, and unworthy of the *farash*. The Hakim prolongs the discussion of Nazu Mia's feet and asks: "Why don't you use shoes?" (Kabir 1945, 16). Without losing his cool, Nazu Mia points to the futility and uselessness of shoes in his peasant life of stress and hardship and associates them with weakness, saying: "Once in a moment of weakness I put on shoes. For seven days I had to limp. We peasants cannot live in cotton wool, Hakim Sahib!" (16). In colonial sartorial conventions, shoes are a mark of modernity and distinction, as Brett A. Berliner (2002) points out: "the wearing of clothes and especially shoes in colonial iconography symbolized the attainment of some level of civilization" (13). Nazu Mia's association of shoes with "weakness" may be intended to expose the deep errancy and fallibility of the colonial system of which the Hakim is a part culturally. It also represents his adherence to local norms, as Fanon states: "The peasant who stays put defends his traditions stubbornly" (1963, 111). In *Men and Rivers*, Nazu Mia upholds his way of life in a comedic tone mixed with seriousness and indignation.

The Hakim's move towards belligerence and hostility directed at Nazu Mia culminates in the question he asks of the latter: "Why don't you at least wash your feet when you are asked to sit on a gentleman's *farash*?" (Kabir 1945, 16). Sensing Nazu Mia's resentment and suppressed (but visible) outrage at this insult, the Hakim seeks to neutralize the conversation by adding: "Shall I ask my man to bring a jug of water for you?" (16). This literally adds insult to the injury already caused by the Hakim's misdemeanour and erodes Nazu Mia's mental composure. Before leaving the shop, Nazu Mia says: "I am a peasant's son and don't know the manners of gentlemen. But we peasants never invite a man and then insult him in our house" (16). Nazu Mia's verbal feat and intellectual triumph help recapture his humanity stolen by colonialism and colonial modernity. In some ways, like Fanon's notion of revolutionary violence, they also function as "some cathartic cleansing and empowering ritual by which to liberate oneself from one's past oppression" (Fanon 1963, 45).

By the contrast between these two modes of manners and behaviour, one represented by Nazu Mia and the other by the Hakim, Kabir celebrates the rustic way of life as opposed to the imported (colonial/bourgeois) gentlemanly sophistication that the outsider Hakim brings to Dhuldi. This goes with Fanon's revolutionary idea of "freeing the colonized mind" and psychologically liberating it (Ranuga 1986, 187). The Hakim's hypocrisy and deceitfulness become more obvious when, after Nazu Mia's departure, he turns to his assistant and scolds him for not removing the *farash* before Nazu Mia's arrival. Having lost any hope of obtaining the crocodile organs and defeated by Nazu Mia's conversational repertoire, the Hakim makes a scapegoat of his assistant in order to save face, maintain self-importance, and retain a modicum of pride and credibility in the eyes of those around him. Thus, he wants to perpetuate the power dialectic and class differences and replicate oppressive systems and attitudes at the expense of the humanity and dignity of the peasants like Nazu Mia.

Conclusion: Cosmopolitan Kabir's peasant leanings

Of Bangladeshi writers in English, Kabir is perhaps the most cosmopolitan. In his lifetime he wielded huge influence politically and intellectually, both locally and internationally. Mainly through his speeches, he had "a significant impact on the academic scenes in Delhi, London, Paris, Madison, and Moscow" (Qureshi 2008, 1140). However, his rootedness in his home soil and in old-world peasant traditions is salient in *Men and Rivers*. Kabir's positive portrayal of the peasantry and the villagers – who constitute the bulk of Bengal's population – is unique in Bangladeshi literature in English. In his portrayal of the rural life of Rahimpur, he celebrates the peasants' human virtues of simplicity, hard work, and bravery and juxtaposes them to the dishonesty and iniquitous conduct of the Dewan and the Hakim who are based in the colonial outpost of Dhuldi and can be compared to the comprador class or privileged colonized subjects who, Fanon believes, identify themselves with, and show allegiance to, colonial culture.

Despite the colonial presence in Dhuldi, the *hat* remains a meeting place for the villagers, and, despite the firmness of the panchayat system in Rahimpur, the villagers are not impervious to colonial control and must pay levies to the Dewan. By extorting taxes from the peasants, the Dewan wrests control of the land of the surrounding areas and riverine islands. Thus Rahimpur and Dhuldi are colonially entangled. However, the two locations chiefly represent two completely opposed systems of rule. Therefore, *Men and Rivers* not only represents Kabir's testament to the moral superiority of the peasants, but is also an exposé of corrupt imperialism embodied by the Dewan (politically and administratively) and the Hakim (culturally). Both characters are colonized locals who promote colonial interests and correspond to Fanon's harsh characterization of the "army of fools" and "imbeciles" who are "the product of a [colonial] psychological-economic system" ([1952] 1986, 35).

Even though colonial centres were carefully planned urban settings, Kabir portrays rural places to demonstrate their impact in the most distant regions of the imperial system and the cultural contact it sustains. Through his depiction of the behaviour of the colonial agents and peasants, he celebrates the Bengali rural way of life with all its humane values as understood and practised by those living in the local community. By comparing the panchayat system of governance with the habits of the colonial administrative official (the Dewan) and cultural product (the Hakim), Kabir shows the ascendancy, pre-eminence, and permanence of local modes of life and customs over imported ones at a time when colonial Bengal witnessed strong peasant political and social movements of which he was a part.

Notes

1. For more details, see Kabir (1960).
2. Semantically, Rahimpur signifies a compassionate valley as embodied by Asgar Mia in the narrative.
3. The distance between Rahimpur and Dhuldi is approximately 5 km.
4. Colonial architecture in Faridpur includes "Faridpur Zilla school (1840), Faridpur court-house (1889), Hitoshi high school (1889), Ishan Institute (1891), Faridpur rail-station (1916), and Rajendra college (1918)" (Turza 2021, 245).
5. An important river port in Bangladesh.

Disclosure statement

No potential conflict of interest was reported by the author.

References

Ahmed, Feroz. 1971. "Why Pakistan's Unity Was Jeopardized?" *Pakistan Forum* 2 (3): 3–6.

Aiyar, Sana. 2008. "Fazlul Huq, Region and Religion in Bengal: The Forgotten Alternative of 1940–43." *Modern Asian Studies* 42 (6): 1213–1249. doi:10.1017/S0026749X07003022.

Amoko, A.O. 2001. "The Problem with English Literature: Canonicity, Citizenship, and the Idea of Africa." *Research in African Literatures* 32 (4): 19–43. doi:10.2979/RAL.2001.32.4.19.

Appiah, Kwame Anthony. 1992. *In My Father's House: Africa in the Philosophy of Culture.* New York: Oxford University Press.

Berliner, Brett A. 2002. *Ambivalent Desire: The Exotic Black Other in Jazz-age France.* Amherst MA: University of Massachusetts Press.

Brown, Ryan. 2010. *The British Empire in India.* Ashland OH: Ashbrook-Ashland University Press.

Choudhury, Shankhadeep. 2002. "Portuguese Family Tree in Bangla Village." *The Times of India,* September 6. https://timesofindia.indiatimes.com/city/kolkata/portuguese-family-tree-in-bangla-village/articleshow/21308355.cms

Davini, Roberto. 2009. "Bengali Raw Silk, the East India Company and the European Global Market, 1770–1833." *Journal of Global History* 4 (1): 57–79. doi:10.1017/S1740022809002952.

Fanon, Frantz. [1952] 1986. *Black Skin, White Masks,* Translated by Charles Lam Markmann. London: Pluto.

Fanon, Frantz. 1963. *The Wretched of the Earth,* Translated by Richard Philcox. New York: Grove Press.

Hasan, Md. Mahmudul. 2022. "Humayun Kabir, *Men and Rivers,* and Faridpur." *The Daily Star,* April 23. https://www.thedailystar.net/star-literature/news/humayun-kabir-men-and-rivers-and-faridpur-3010491

Husain, Syed Sajjad. [1994] 2022. *Civilization and Society.* Dhaka: Academia Publishing House.

Iyer, Pushpa, and Merrick Hoben. 2018. "Working through Cultural Changes: Community Conflicts in India." In *Cultural Encounters and Emergent Practices in Conflict Resolution Capacity-Building,* edited by Tamra Pearson d'Estrée and Ruth J. Parsons, 215–237. New York: Palgrave Macmillan.

Jaffe, James A. 2014. "Custom, Identity, and the Jury in India, 1800–1832." *The Historical Journal* 57 (1): 131–155. doi:10.1017/S0018246X13000435.

Jones, M.E. Monckton. 1920. "Review of *Dupleix and Clive; the Beginning of Empire* by Henry Dodwell." *The English Historical Review* 35 (140): 605–609. doi:10.1093/ehr/XXXV.CXL.605.

Kabir, Humayun. 1945. *Men and Rivers.* Bombay: Hind Kitabs.

Kabir, Humayun. 1960. "Congress Ideology: A Statement." *India Quarterly* 16 (1): 2–23. doi:10.1177/097492846001600101.

Kabir, Humayun. 1968. *The Bengali Novel.* Calcutta: Firma K. L. Mukhopadhyay.

Lazarus, Neil. 1993."Disavowing. "Decolonization: Fanon, Nationalism, and the Problematic of Representation in Current Theories of Colonial Discourse." *Research in African Literatures* 24 (4): 69–98.
Mircea, Flaviu. 2019. "Signage through the Ages". *Medium*, January 15. https://medium.com/@flaviu.mirc/signage-through-the-ages-9e5e8bc06d25
Novak, James J. 1993. *Bangladesh: Reflections on the Water.* Bloomington, IN: Indiana University Press.
Pandya, Sameer Praful. 2001. *The Late Colonial Self: The Nationalist Autobiography in India, 1927–1951.* PhD diss, Stanford University.
Pratt, Mary Louise. 1992. *Imperial Eyes: Travel Writing and Transculturation.* New York: Routledge.
Qureshi, Mahmud Shah. 2008. "Literary Assessments of Tagore by Bengali Muslim Writers." *University of Toronto Quarterly* 77 (4): 1133–1152. doi:10.3138/utq.77.4.1133.
Ranuga, Thomas K. 1986. "Frantz Fanon and Black Consciousness in Azania (South Africa)." *Phylon (1960-)* 47 (3): 182–191. doi:10.2307/274985.
Rashiduzzaman, M. 1970. "The Awami League in the Political Development of Pakistan." *Asian Survey* 10 (7): 574–587. doi:10.2307/2642956.
Salleh, Suhaimi, and Noraini Abdullah. 2017. "Observation on Signboard Photographs in Kota Kinabalu, Sabah as Indicator of Change Towards Global Business." *Journal of Global Business and Social Entrepreneurship (GBSE)* 1 (4): 35–44.
Sharma, Neelam. 2004. "Oldest Harappan Signboard at Kutch Township". *The Times of India*, February 19. https://timesofindia.indiatimes.com/city/chandigarh/oldest-harappan-signboard-at-kutch-township/articleshow/505144.cms?from=mdr
Spivak, Gayatri C. 1988. "Can the Subaltern Speak?" In *Marxism and the Interpretation of Culture*, edited by C. Nelson and L. Grossberg, 271–313. Chicago: University of Illinois Press.
Spivak, Gayatri C. 1990. "Questions of Multiculturalism." In *The Post-Colonial Critic: Interviews, Strategies, Dialogues*, edited by Sara Harasym, 59–66. New York: Routledge.
Steel, Tim. 2015. "Portuguese Bangladesh." *Dhaka Tribune*, September 11. https://archive.dhakatribune.com/uncategorized/2015/09/11/portuguese-bangladesh
Turza, Asif Ibney Basit. 2021. "Sustainable Urban Form and Dynamics of Rivers in the Context of Faridpur City, Bangladesh." In *Resilient and Responsible Smart Cities*, edited by Norsidah Ujang, Tomohiro Fukuda, Anna Laura Pisello, and Dinko Vukadinović, 243–254. Cham: Springer.
Varghese, V.J. 2009. "Land, Labour and Migrations: Understanding Kerala's Economic Modernity." (Working paper). Thiruvananthapuram: Centre for Development Studies.
Vincentnathan, S. George. 2001. "Review of *Disputes and Arguments Amongst Nomads: A Caste Council in India*, by Robert M. Hayden." *Journal of Political Ecology* 8 (1): 29–32.

"Here I'll stay": Kaiser Haq's poems and the impact of being at home

Kathryn Hummel

ABSTRACT

This article examines the choice of celebrated Bangladeshi anglophone poet and scholar Kaiser Haq (b. 1950) to remain in, rather than migrate from, his home country, despite significant career-related travel abroad and an international literary presence. In Haq's poem "Published in the Streets of Dhaka", the speaker declares: "I was born and live here", an assertion of "staying" in Bangladesh that reflects Haq's positionality and guides the explorations in this article. Through an analysis of selected poems from the 1970s to the present day, the discussion highlights the sensory, sociopolitical, and postcolonial detail that arises from Haq's continual close interaction with his place as a dynamic milieu, rather than a remembered or physically distant ancestral land. This sense of his presence, which involves an observational approach here compared to that of an anthropologist, enhances the nuances of Kaiser Haq's identity as a "local" to and in Bangladesh and his concurrent transnational gaze.

Introduction: The qualities of distance

The influence of distance in literature varies, naturally, depending on circumstance. While Edward Said (2012) underlines its effect on the political and creative output of the "poet in exile" (138), Ha Jin (2008) reflects that removal from an ancestral land "often deprives [migrants] of a sense of direction and prevents them from putting down roots anywhere" (63). Carine Mardorossian (2002) observes that the distance of the exiled writer from their country allows for "an 'objective' view of the two worlds they are straddling [...]. They are ascribed the status of neutral observers, a detachment on which [...] their literary authority is based" (16). Kaiser Haq, "arguably the most internationally renowned Bangladeshi poet in the English language" (2021, 136), diverges from the writer in exile by writing, translating, and pursuing scholarship from Bangladesh. He thus contemplates distance through references to the temporal, cultural, environmental, and political more than a spatial removal from his place of origin. If anything, Haq's published works of poetry from 1978 to the present might be considered the poetry of staying put, or simply "staying" – in contrast to the writings of the Bangladeshi diaspora largely concerned with "space travelled, experienced and registered as [physical] distance" (Lee 2015, 133). While these writings may emphasize "memory, nostalgia and ideals" (Mand 2010, 278), as in *A Golden Age* by Bangladeshi-born British writer Tahmima Anam (2008), with its passages describing pre-independence prosperity and domestic tranquillity in Dhaka, they can also, as Maswood Akhter (2017) notes of *Seasonal Adjustments* by Bangladeshi-born, Australian-based novelist Adib Khan (1994), adopt a distinctly dystopian tone that serves "as a useful interrogation, even necessary resistance, to insular/parochial romanticization of 'home'" (Akhter 2017, 151).

For Haq, staying implies neither insularity nor stasis, as the first section of this article explores. Given Rebecca Walkowitz's (2006) statement that "not every book that travels is produced by a writer who travels" (532), Haq's predominantly Bangladesh-based output demonstrates a sensitivity to context that flourishes with staying. The themes, forms, and language of his work heighten the nuances of Haq's identity as a Bangladeshi local and his concurrent transnational gaze and presence.

As discussed in the second section, Haq's poetry is often distinguished by wry expressions of both postcolonial resistance to yet solidarity with the cultures of Bangladesh. In his poem "Published in the Streets of Dhaka", also the title proper of Haq's (2007c) *Collected Poems, 1966–2006*, the speaker declares: "I was born and live here" (31), significantly asserting the legitimacy and necessity of the right to write from a country regarded, as intimated by the poem's epigraph, as an absurd province from the (notably western) outsider's point of view. Haq's frequent return to such themes from his base in Bangladesh is thus considered as another outcome of his inclination to stay.

In the third section, Haq's poetry and his location will be considered from the perspective of anthropology and its emphasis on the close observation of everyday life. As suggested by the appellation of "anthropoet", Haq's keen perceptive abilities and empathy give rise to the richness of sensory, social, and historic detail in his poetry. While this immersion has led Radha Chakravarty to comment that Haq's poems construct "a distinctively Bangladeshi reality" (Chakravarty 2008) here it is argued, with reference to self-reflexive ethnographic methodology (Ellingson 2009), that staying accords Haq the opportunity to "plumb" a subjective centre (Haq 2007c, 31). In this instance, "staying" also implies the continual observation of and interaction with one's surroundings as a dynamic and developing milieu, rather than a remembered or physically distant ancestral land.

The transnational local

Despite his demonstrated preference for staying in Bangladesh, Haq's career has nevertheless been marked by various forms of journeying: not only for PhD studies at the University of Warwick and subsequent fellowships and residencies abroad, but through the geopolitical shift from East Pakistan to Bangladesh during his lifetime. The establishment of the People's Republic of Bangladesh after the Liberation War with (West) Pakistan in 1971, and its often conflicting currents of religion, culture, and language, make for a complex national identity, as Partha Ghosh (1993) notes:

> If Bangladesh asserts its Islamic identity, it cannot justify its liberation struggle, as that was not only directed against Islamic Pakistan but was actively aided by "Hindu" India. Alternatively, if it displays its Bengali credentials, it runs the risk of merging its identity beyond recognition into that of West Bengal and its major city, Calcutta, the cultural capital

> for all Bengalis in India and abroad. Even a simultaneous assertion of Bengali and Islamic identities serves only a limited purpose because this does not satisfactorily distinguish Bangladesh from West Bengal. (699)

The unease Ghosh describes is reflected in Haq's poem "Pariah", in which the speaker observes a process of change to both his personal and national identity, aligning to Pico Iyer's (1988) claim that places do "to some extent remake us, recast us in their own images" and "tell us as much about them as about ourselves" (26). The first change is portrayed through the plight of a childhood friend who at first distinguishes himself as a "leader" (Haq 2017, 52), relying on his sharp wit and playful antics to win the affections and following of his peers. The boys are portrayed as a pack, ominously likened in the first stanza to street-smart stray dogs "making friends with the dust of hostile streets" (52).

"Pariah" is a narrative of disintegration – of childhood, seemingly experienced in the 1950s era of Haq's own, and its rough democracy. The speaker, who briefly refers to his middle-class signifier of "anglophone school" (Haq 2017, 52), idolizes an older boy of keen wit who becomes a wage-earner in "his dead father's office", replete with "plans to acquire higher power" (53). The strain behind these developments is suggested by the leader's laughter, described as "more manic than ever", but, for the moment, still appealing (53). Similarly implied is the misfit between the leader's, or Pariah's, essential nature and the roles expected of him, roles that ultimately lead to unemployment, desperation, and withdrawal. Haq's precise choice of the oxymoronic "safety blade" as the Pariah's tool of attempted suicide reflects the confusion of a space in which young men and stray dogs struggle for survival (53). The final stanza of "Pariah" explores the alienation from the familiar due to the violence of progress, referencing the wider surroundings in which both the speaker and his erstwhile leader live as young adults:

> and demonstrators ran into police bullets
> and genocidal wars spread like brush fire
> and refugees filled up maps
> and independence lit up the sky with fireworks
> and varieties of misrule flourished
> and slums grew like leaves in spring
> (54–55)

Depicted in "Pariah" through the lens of childhood streetside adventuring and, later, the havoc wrought by unrest, the influence of place on Haq's poetic identity is noted by Chakravarty (2008) in her review of Haq's 2007 collection *Published in the Streets of Dhaka*. The apparently contradictory "range of ideas, emotions and experiences" in the volume connotes

> the voice of the poet himself, at once rooted in the local context and at home in the world at large. His fragmented persona, dispersed across a profusion of poems, makes it difficult to categorize Kaiser Haq's poetry with easy labels. (n.p.)

In discussing the ebb and flow of "multiple labels and identities" attributed to mainly "Asian, African and Caribbean writers", Haq cites the "third-world writer, a postcolonial or a postmodern writer", but notably omits the transnational writer – even though the term likewise enables "critics to focus on a body of writing that would otherwise have been in a limbo" (2007a). Situating Haq's work in a "culture" of transnationalism rather than the mere "global cultural conditions that facilitated the formation of transnational networks" (Hage 2017, 192) transforms limbo into connectivity across "national borders, language, and literary and critical traditions" (Seyhan 2000, xviii). Underlining the significance of Haq's transnational voice, Chakravarty goes on to cite Haq's 1978 poem "Growing Up or Softly Falling" in which the speaker, ostensibly a reflection of Haq, describes his own being as

> schizoid,
> split
> between this and that,
> between my western know-how
> and eastern wisdom,
> between that and this,
> forever falling
> between two silly stools in a proverb
> (Haq 2007c, 64–65)

This split speaks to an identity based on polarities; however, the constant risk of falling suggests there is an alternative space "where one is inside and outside at the same time" (Featherstone and Lash 1999, 10), a transnational existence predicated on borderlessness, despite or even without a distinct point of rootedness or belonging. If "this and that" denotes colonial and postcolonial spaces (Haq 2007c, 64–65), then the space in between evokes the concept of hybridity, a co-characteristic of transnationalism that allows for the re-formation of identity and discourse in reaction to colonial influence (Mercer 1992).

Haq reflects on his habitation of this in-between space by controversially likening himself to a "hijra" (transgender) person, one who belongs "neither to one category or another", in order to "describe the status of Bangladeshi writers in English" (2021, 138). Eschewing further appropriation, Haq goes on to explain that "there is no officially recognized place for English in [Bangladesh]. It is the de facto second language of the educated classes, but the constitution regards it as a foreign language" (139). While Haq identifies his strong relation "to the tradition of South Asian Anglophone writing" as the major influence that distinguishes his work from literary peers writing in Bangla (139), he concedes a "shared sensibility" of culture and context that simply finds "expression in Bengali in my friends' works, and in English in mine" (139).

Much of Haq's poetry simultaneously acknowledges the plurality of identity with the shifts of and between space and place, recognizing that experiences of both involve a series of literal and figurative "uprootings/regroundings" (Ahmed et al. 2003, 3); allowing for various developments between one's "place of origin" and one's "lived experience" (Brah 1996, 186), whether across geographic distance or not. One such piece, the prose poem "Forever Amber", focuses on the transitions that occur within the particular location of Dhaka: "Rich, poor, the layers in between – all are out in the city streets everyday" (Haq 2017, 42).

This portrayal of plurality is a humanitarian response, perhaps the only tenable one for a poet living in a country "rived by the two divisive political identities [...] the first based on language and the latter on religion" (Hajjaj 2020, 1). This division is attributed to the contesting ideologies of Bangladesh's leading political parties: the Awami League, with its emphasis on a language-based, "Bengali" identity distinct from pre-liberation Pakistan (2), and the Bangladesh Nationalist Party (BNP), which in 1977 "kindled a new form of religion-based identity [...], coining it Bangladeshi nationalism" (1), further compounding the "latent tension between the [constitutional] idea of secularism and the role of religion" in Bangladesh (Riaz 2009, 82). Aptly, in "Forever Amber", Haq's observation of Dhaka's notoriously tangled flow of traffic becomes an image for Bangladesh's "state of governance, whichever party holds power" (2017, 42): "Mercedes, BMW, Lexus. Battered public buses, motorized three-wheelers, rickshaws, pedal vans. All in a scramble, like dogs nosing each others' bottoms, sometimes in the wrong direction" (42).

Despite these sly metaphors, Haq (2018, n.p.) claims not to be "a political writer" but an attendant of everyday detail, in which politics is swiftly being overtaken by economic concerns. This claim stems from Haq abjuring Bangladesh's partisan political structure, to which he cannot respond in a "literary context without being at once placed within that [...] framework" (2018, n.p.). While Jin writes that the "worst crime the country commits against the writer is to make [... them] unable to write with honesty and artistic integrity" (Jin 2008), in Haq's poems this truncation can be discerned through a recurring tone that one may assume to be Haq's own, or at least that of his poetic counterpart: a tone of weariness in reaction to the dismal progress and events narrated. Elsewhere, Haq admits another reaction in the forms of "satire and social criticism" which he considers

> to be the most significant aspects of literature in the world today. I couldn't be mystical or philosophical even if I tried. When I focus on the self, it is a self beleaguered by everything that is rotten in the state of the world. (2021, 143)

In "Kabbadi with Death", written after the murder of Biswajit Das by Chhatra League activists protesting a December 2012 *hartal* (strike) in Dhaka,[1] the speaker critiques the misguided political violence behind the act and dwells on the practical and humane: "What happens to the ash / From burnt young flesh / Disinfected of politics" (Haq 2017, 58). While any empathy in the poem is reserved for Das, mistaken by his assailants for a supporter of the opposition BNP, Haq's pragmatic tone is repeated in "Getting it Right", as the speaker reflects on the frequent and often ineffective *hartals*: "in prose or verse / It'd come out the same: / Day 9 of blockade, / Eight more dead" (40).

When called upon to address his preference for English as his literary language, Haq (2008) asserts another hybrid: a fusion of the romantic and rational parts of his Bangladeshi psyche, realized through writing in English. This form of hybridity is evident not only in the politics of detached compassion in his poetry, but in Haq's blending of literary traditions, a practice that articulates his transnational grasp if not appeal. Mafruha Mohua (2020) views Haq's writing as reflecting the deep influence of both Bengali and Anglo European literary traditions (533), citing Haq's "A Late Poem" which gracefully moves from "distinctly Dhaka imagery to Greek mythology to an echo of King Lear" (533). Such bricolage is not, of course, unusual in poetry, yet, more than being just a feature of Haq's craft, it speaks to his location and placement of identity. Ghassan Hage (2017) notes that it

> is striking how, in reading the available literature on migration, one is left with an implicit impression that cultural complexity and hybridity are always on the side of the cultures of destination while the villages immigrants leave are imagined to be simple and monocultural. (196)

Haq's works likewise demonstrate that staying in Bangladesh does not preclude the cultures or identities of transnationalism. In conversation, Haq has reflected on what he describes as the "road not taken", a plan for migration to New Zealand abandoned after the death of his first wife in 1999:

> I remained [... in Bangladesh]. But throughout all this, whatever I have written has been rooted here and at the same time it has been the work of someone who is open to experience, open to the world, ideas and influences from everywhere. (2018, n.p.)

Here Haq compounds Walkowitz's (2006, 534) idea of the non-immigrant writer who, while "staying", is engaged "intellectually with the movement of people and objects across geographies and cultures" and thus simultaneously experiences belonging and border-crossing; the local as well as transnational. Accordingly, while discussing his fragmented approach to memoir, Haq inadvertently demonstrates the international reach and appeal of his works, pointing to publications and publishers in India, the UK, and Bangladesh:

> I have published another memoir titled "Testament of a Pseudo-Translator" in a journal in Odisha; and an autobiographical essay on my experience of our food culture has come out from Pan Macmillan Picador India and Beacon Books (UK) in an anthology titled *Desi Delicacies*, edited by Claire Chambers (2020). There was an essay in *London Magazine* in 1986 that is a sort of intellectual autobiography; and an essay titled "Karl Marx vs. Nux Vomica 200" in *Bengal Lights* (Haq 2012) that would fit into a memoir. I published a memoir of Berlin on the eve of reunification in the Edinburgh journal *Chapman*. (2021, 149)

Haq directly cites "increasing transnationality" as an inevitable outcome of a "globalized world" characterized by greater mobility and migration (2021, 141–142). He therefore makes a case for his own positionality as well as that of diasporic writers when he suggests writing be judged "on its merits" rather than the "mother tongue or nationality" of the author, or whether it is a "diaspora text or something produced in the motherland" (142). As a transnational local, Haq's is arguably a plural mode of habitation and identity that exists in defiance of the binaries that gave impetus to their forms.

"Plumb in the centre": Haq's postcolonial Bangladesh

If the regimes of truth produced by colonial history are mimicked in discursive practice, one role of postcolonial discourse, including and perhaps most particularly literature, is to detach "the power of truth from the forms of hegemony, social, economic and cultural, within which it operates" (Foucault 1972, 133). This process often involves the re-examinations and re-presentations of the colonial condition (Suleri 1992), one that established Anglo European colonial culture as superior, and erased or otherwise diminished – physically, culturally, and discursively – those colonized. This process of interrogation of colonial discourse and its re-presentation as postcolonial is often prominent, not the least by virtue of his staying in Bangladesh, in the poetry of Haq.

"Published in the Streets of Dhaka" (Haq 2007c, 30) is one such poem that addresses this structure of dominating and dominated cultures. In Haq's own words, the poem is a "declaration of literary independence" (2021, 149), one that challenges the prevailing colonial dichotomy outlined above. The poem is prefaced by an epigraph from Gore

Vidal, taken from an apparently self-deprecating anecdote about a vocabulary-related blunder. While Vidal contemplates his story circulating first to nearby Fitzrovia and then far-flung Dhaka, for Haq the Bangladesh reference serves as a point of bantering protest:

> That's a stretch! I should know,
> I was born and live here.
> Your pretty tale swinging into print
> Under the bamboo, the banyan and the mango tree
> Is the height of absurdity – isn't that your point?
> (2007c, 30)

While the second line of the stanza reinforces Haq's identity with place, as discussed earlier, here the assertion takes a different tone: those from or inside Dhaka's absurd outpost are the only ones who may jibe at it, in the grand tradition of identity-related slurs, without it being seen as a "snide / aside" (31). The poem goes through modes of satire ("After all, Mr. Gore Vidal, / You are almost as famous / As Vidal Sassoon") and self-satire ("lyric verse and motley belles lettres / Peep out of routine stacks of Exam Guides / Like rusty needles – I too have perpetrated a few") before a keen outpouring of rhetorical questions:

> What are we to do, Mr. Vidal?
> Stop writing, and if we do, not publish?
> Join an immigration queue, hoping
> One day to head for the Diaspora dead-end,
> An exhibit in an alien multicultural museum? (31)

By pointing out the elitism of remote literary scenes in the west, Haq also asserts the legitimacy of the local: the Bangladeshi writers who persevere with their craft, as well as the writers who stay rather than opt for a path of immigration and possible tokenism in foreign settings, or engage in a commodification of the "exotic" homeland in their works (Akhter 2017, 162). Previously, Haq has expressed his tenacity regarding both staying and writing as a means to evolution: "I do feel things can drive you out of your country but I do want a certain kind of life to be possible here. A literary life, a lively literary scene – that is missing [from Bangladesh] now" (2018, n.p.). Such revival is not only the job of the lone writer but of a community, as Walkowitz suggests: "the location of literature depends not only on the places where books are written" but also on the places where they are "classified and given social purpose" (2006, 527). In "Published in the Streets of Dhaka", as in life, Haq makes an argument for staying; for the vitality and significance of local literature to its place of conception and consumption, from the "bazaar booksellers" to the city streets (2007c, 30), and beyond.

Poulomi Saha alludes to the tenuousness of Bangladesh's literary identity by describing the former East Bengal as "subsumed" frequently by West Bengal (India) and rendered culturally indistinct; at other times "romanticized as the [...] source of raw material and poetic feeling" that continues to serve the "urban political intelligentsia" centred in Kolkata (quoted in Mohua 2020, 529). Haq himself has noted that writers in Bangladesh had to be "retroactively enfranchised" after independence in 1971 (quoted in Mohua 2020, 528), aligning themselves to a new geopolitical entity and national identity while a sense of enduring culture and community remained, ravaged but intact. "Published in the Streets of Dhaka" notably contains the declaration: "Here I'll stay, plumb in the center / Of monsoon-mad Bengal" (Haq 2007c, 31). Yet what is the "center" to which the speaker refers? Haq's use of "Bengal" suggests the ambiguity of human-designed borders after the Partition of India in 1947 and of a community that is ethno-cultural; where kinship is defined by, amongst other factors, language (Hajjaj 2020, 3). Strikingly, the "famous predecessor" mentioned in the same stanza can be identified as Jibanananda Das (Haq 2007c, 31), a pre-modernist poet claimed by both "sides" of Bengal, with his birthplace in Barisal, Bangladesh and death in Kolkata, India.

The speaker cuts through romanticized notions of the "streets of Dhaka" by noting their troubled reality, replete with "flashing knives, whirling sticks, bursting bombs, / And accompanying gutturals and fricatives of hate", as well as the ubiquitous "evil" (Haq 2007c, 31), all of which may be recorded and disseminated by the writer remaining amongst them. While Chakravarty interprets the poem as narrating a transition "from an anguished sense of being in-between cultures" to a "confident acceptance of [Haq's] place in the world" (Chakravarty 2008), the constant awareness of the local's gaze on Dhaka and its streets, and the assured belief in the legitimacy of staying and writing from them, is both a challenge to and reconceptualization of "space and identity" (Mardorossian 2002, 22). In "Published in the Streets of Dhaka", Haq foregrounds "ambivalence, fragmentation, and plurality" in elements as diverse as literary talent to malevolent forces (Mardorossian 2002, 22). Most of all, Haq expresses the sense of having been born of these liminal qualities; then choosing to stay and explore.

A similar analysis of postcolonial location, though decidedly more wistful, is Haq's (2017) poem "Santahar" (15). Although the railway town of Santahar is located in Bangladesh, it exists in the speaker's consciousness as a paradoxically obtainable "private vice" (16). Having been "forged in the furnace" of the British Raj before the Partition of India in 1947 (16), Santahar's historic function as a rail connection to Siliguri in West Bengal is recalled, whereas the description "stained / with the blood of history" alludes to the 1971 massacre of Santahar's Bihari residents by the Bangladeshi guerrilla resistance force Mukti Bahini or freedom fighters (Haq 2017, 16; Kamrani 2017). While contemporary Santahar is described a site of "everyday life" for the people connecting through its train line, for the poem's speaker the town still serves as a fantasy destination with "magic" in its name (Haq 2017, 16).

The appeal of Santahar lies somewhat in its unexplored proximity, an accessibility that has never been grasped in actuality, since the speaker's desire to visit is revealed as an idle thought: "I must go there one of these days, / I say to myself, and lazily / Google it on YouTube" (Haq 2017, 16). Yet the fact that Santahar is the subject of a poem or online video signals its significance to the insider's consciousness, again indicating the plurality of belonging that includes both the mundane and particular. "Santahar" is thus a poem of a distinctly interior view, in contrast to the ridiculing outsider's gaze of "Published in the Streets of Dhaka", thereby reworking the colonial discourse described in *The Post-Colonial Critic* by Gayatri Spivak and Sarah Harasym (1990). Since what is accepted as "authenticity" is "constructed by hegemonic voices" of colonialism, resistance comes with "[teasing] out is what is not there" or not immediately evident under this homogenizing influence (61). At the end of the poem, Santahar is transmuted into a location symbolic of longing and belonging, a meaning interchangeable with various seemingly unremarkable places yet reliant on the subjectivity of the beholder: "it's any place you want to go back to / so you can die in peace" (Haq 2017, 17). If the postcolonial writer inscribes "history from below" the prevalent discourse (Choudhury 2013, 62), Haq achieves a similar effect by writing from the inside.

In describing the interplay of the dominant Occident and the submissive Orient, Said ([1978] 2003) emphasizes the intractability of identity and positioning within structures of colonial power:

> No one has ever devised a method for detaching the [individual] from the circumstances of life, from the fact of [... their] involvement (conscious or unconscious) with a class, a set of beliefs, a social position, or from the mere activity of being a member of a society. (10)

Haq's assertions and experiences of staying in Bangladesh position him as a member of its society, yet one whose roles are varied, and whose voice is polyphonic. Haq's choice of English as a linguistic medium, discussed above, also calls forth Homi Bhabha's (1985) concept of mimicry, in which the colonized adopts the colonizer's language, undermining the latter's authority by creating opportunities for "signs of spectacular resistance" (104). Seen through the lens of transnationalism, Haq's resistance includes the "freedom to experiment and invent a modern voice unburdened by many [...] national conditionings and anxieties" (Zecchini 2017, 49), yet a voice nevertheless engaged in observation of global systems and local impact.

Haq's (2007b) "Ode on the Lungi" is a renowned address on issues of marginality, hegemony, and social exclusion "caused by a fragmented postcolonial world" (Choudhury 2013, 61). Haq's subject is the ubiquitous lungi, a symbol of local or even subaltern identity that, like language, is not easily translated, even as it is worn in a multiplicity of guises around the world:

> Hundreds of millions
> from East Africa to Indonesia
> wear the lungi, also known variously
> as the sarong, munda, htamain, saaram,
> ma'awaiis, kitenge, kanga, kaiki
> They wear it day in day out,
> indoors and out
> Just think –
> at any one moment
> there are more people in lungis
> than the population of the USA
> (2007b, n.p.)

Despite this global reach, "sartorial [in]equality" remains (n.p.), just as wider social and economic inequality does between the "advanced West and the backward non-West" in the poem's mapping of the postcolonial world (Chakravarty 2008 n.p.). Haq's habitual eye for detail travels beyond the local, citing the example of hegemony in the "private space" of a cousin's home in the US, where the lungi is banished by the cousin's son for being "'ridiculous ethnic attire'" (2007b, n.p.). Haq's subsequent line, "I AM A LUNGI ACTIVIST!", has the same knowing resonance of "Here I'll stay" (2007c, 31), yet Haq goes further here to convince readers of the reasons for his championship of the garment, with several stanzas devoted to detailed celebration of the lungi in a broadly good-humoured tone. Nevertheless, lines appear to punctuate his hyperbole, situating the poem as protest against detractors of the lungi and the culture/s it represents:

In short
the lungi is a complete wardrobe
for anyone interested:
an emblem of egalitarianism,
symbol of global left-outs
Raised and flapped amidst laughter
it's the subaltern speaking
(Haq 2007b, n.p.)

Although Haq's use of the literary language of English allows his poetry to travel beyond the place where he stays, the poem's withering final line, directed at those who maintain their "indisposition" towards the lungi and its wearers, excluding more than a garment, is evidently not an attempt to "bridge cultural frontiers" (Chakravarty 2008, n.p.). Rather, it is once more an assertion of the erudite local whose critique of colonialism's continuing legacy is so keen, a rejoinder may not be called for or even necessary.

"Being there": The anthropoet

In regard to Haq's (2018) observation of poets as generally gregarious types, it follows that the poet is a keen observer as well as participant in life. Participant-observation is a method most often aligned to anthropology, yet serves for anyone engaging in a life characterized by a highly tuned awareness: "on the one hand grasping the sense of specific occurrences and gestures empathetically, on the other stepping back to situate these meanings in wider contexts" (Clifford 1983, 127). The anthropologist and the poet are described as asking the same questions about people, culture, and themselves as actors, only with differing approaches (Daniel 1989). For the anthropologist, "being there" means entering a new culture and staying for long enough to penetrate at the desired level for gathering knowledge (Geertz 1988, 5); for Haq, "being there" is not transient but an ostensibly life-long commitment to an already familiar "field" – to which his poetry, as detailed commentary, attests.

Haq's poetry is immersed and immersive, drawing on what James Clifford refers to as "the dialectic of experience and interpretation" (1983, 127). This deep involvement in the arterial life of Dhaka is apparent in "An English Sonnet = 140 Syllables" (Haq 2016, n.p.), whose epigraph from John Gray's *Straw Dogs* ("Can we not think of the aim of life as being simply to see?") indicates the inescapable act of observation, of watching "the passing show" with or without conscious response (Haq 2016). The poem opens with the unfolding of the day's news:

Blinkingly you read –
A poet's retraction
Of satirical verses –
Headlines packed with lies –
Hear the growl of motorbike –
Killer or cop – who knows –
While the perennial masque goes on
For those who've made a killing –
(Haq 2016, n.p.)

Just as the structure of the poem, a response to Shakespeare's Sonnet 66, is tersely lined and contemporary, broken with dashes, so too are the references to the "social evils, corruption and misuse of power" (Choudhury 2013, 61). The strangled voices of literature and the media, the violence that takes multitudinous forms, and the opacity of the tirelessly greedy are all hallmarks of modern-day Bangladesh to the speaker who watches everything become "a tad worse / Each morning" (Haq 2016, n.p.). What is left but to "take note of things", to bear witness even from an inescapably obscured vantage point: "So what if one can't tell / Substance from shadow – " (n.p.). In this way, Haq's local perspective is aligned with the traditional anthropologist's role of participant-observer and the modern anthropologist's admittance of the subjective lens through which they gaze (Ellingson 2009, 13–14).

The bleakness of the view in "An English Sonnet", compared to Haq's rambunctious satirical works, suggests that poetry can indeed be a source of the "historical" and "precise" (Van Maanen 1988, 101), or at least a record of note. In Haq's (2007c) poem "Your Excellency", the speaker admits that poetry "[m]ay not be the verb / In the grammar of dissent" but functions to, again, distil the outcomes of observing and thinking (131). Similarly, "A to Z, Azad", dedicated to the memory of writer, linguist, and professor Humayun Azad, "who was attacked by Islamic militants for writing a scathing satire against them", reinforces the significance of participant-observation and writing as testament (Chakravarty 2008, n.p.), with less emphasis on literary aspirations: "My subject is Life, and the protest / against the enemies of Life. / The Poetry is in the Protest" (Haq 2007c, 12).

In anthropological style, Haq "privileges the body as a site of knowing" over physical distance or the distance of memory (Conquergood 1991, 180), by way of connecting more deeply to the contexts he depicts. "As Usual" commences with another everyday Dhaka scene, a meeting between friends for *cha* and *adda* (tea and chat). While the literal body is neither described nor signified, the sparsely descriptive stanzas connect the physical presence of the speaker and his friend to the familiar, immersive site of the tea stall:

As usual
My old friend
The Sage of the Roadside Tea-stall
Casually solves a problem or two
Between sips of semi-viscous tea
For which, as usual, I am paying
Because, as usual, he is out of pocket.
(Haq 2007c, 27)

Although the revelations expounded by the speaker's friend on the abolition of greed and power allow Haq to indulge in a volley of minute wordplay ("No taka–no trickery, / No pounds sterling–no pound of flesh, / No moolah–no murder"), it is the act of meeting, of drinking tea, and of conversing that accords the poem its situational ambience (27). In "Eid Mubarak" (Haq n.d.), the speaker is concerned with highly sensual, remembered detail in preference to the present bleak outlook for the holiday:

The bustle in the kitchen
the syrupy sweet dish
and the chicken-pilau
The early morning bathe

the new clothes
with their pleasant factory smell
and cotton wads
soused in attar of roses
in the ear
The callisthenics
of collective prayer
the criss-cross hugs
to a count of three
the coins dispensed
to chanting beggars.

With its minute rendering of celebrations past, the poem "Eid Mubarak" stands as an example of an "artifact" that not only "reflects but also forges culture" as it refers to a festival repeated annually (Jin 2008, 17) with variations, giving opportunity to both create and recreate the atmosphere of Eid and its celebration. Moreover, it stands as "a testimony" to the act of staying (Cheung 2012, 4), and to the existential ponderings of a past occasion simultaneously experienced in the present.

"Eid Mubarak" also reflects the voice of an individual, who, while physically present in the place of writing, appears affected by lassitude caused not by trauma but staying. To apply Jin's reflection to Haq's situation: inevitably the poet "has changed and so has his memory of his homeland" but "his homeland has also changed, no longer matching his memory of it [... .] [O]ne cannot return to the same place as the same person" (Jin's 2008). These changes, in Haq's case, may be taken as the shift from East Pakistan to Bangladesh during his undergraduate years, as well as the changes wrought by the progression of time and social life. If, as Chakravarty notes above, Haq's poems "construct a distinctively Bangladeshi reality" (Chakravarty 2008 n.p.), "being there", or staying there, is a worthy pursuit, merging as it does the identities of the "writer as social being" and "writer who writes" (Jin 2008, 29). In Haq's poetry, there is proximity and there is distance; there is a sense of having been too long a standing witness to the vicissitudinal actions and reactions of humanity. Yet while anthropologists always have the choice of retreat from such immersion, the poet stays.

Conclusion: Haq at home

At the conclusion of Haq's "An English Sonnet", the reader is left with the sense that the speaker cannot quite believe that they have survived the staying. "To face the tide is folly", Haq writes, "But if you'll join me / Together we'll take note of things / So long as we can breathe – [...] Call it love / Or what you will" (Haq 2016, n.p.). Removed from more bellicose articulations of nostalgia and nationalism, Haq's poetry imparts a plural perspective of what it means to stay put, interpret, and articulate immediate and unfolding realities. Although staying in Bangladesh was for Haq ostensibly neither a political statement nor an embodied protest against the repercussions of colonialism, his decision is marked by an absence of the "ambivalence that is foundational to the diasporic condition" (Hage 2017, 201); that is, the vacillation between staying and leaving, in mind if not in body, even after departure from one's homeland.

"When home becomes a series of mental images or a mythic space of desire", writes Akhter, "it automatically ceases to be a place of any real return" (2017, 152). Without the distraction of an imagined or realized homecoming, Haq's poetry has instead grown within and expanded beyond the places and experiences in which it is immersed but not always rooted. Be it as the hybridized author of a body of work within transnational literature or simply as a human being characterized by the outcomes of inevitable existential decisions, Haq's immersive detail and socially critical perception demonstrates he remains simultaneously engaged at home and away. Haq's idiosyncratic identity of "urbane wordsmith immersed in his craft" and defending the legitimacy of his stance to a "postcolonial" world, combined with the "ironic observer" detached from his process (Chakravarty 2008, n.p.), is inevitably bound to his locality. Not to be overlooked is the private persona behind the speaker, a mask in its own way but one also firmly positioned in Bangladesh.

Through Haq's poetry, readers are granted space to examine what drives others to leave while some stay: our own places are magnified by his wide gaze and accomplished arrangements of words. Haq at home is transformative; through his gaze, home itself becomes less bound by its deceptively comforting but insidious roots. Haq decentralizes our eye – through which, as through his poetry, we might learn and evolve.

Note

1. On December 9, 20,212, 24-year-old Biswajit Das, "proprietor of Amantron Tailors in the capital's Shakharibazar, was hacked to death on his way to the tailoring shop during a countrywide road blockade" (Khan 2017, n.p.). The blockade, instigated by the 18 Party Alliance led by the Bangladesh Nationalist Party, drew protest from the opposition party Awami League and its student activist wing, the Bangladesh Chhatra League (BCL). Members of BCL from Jagannath University attacked Das "with machetes, iron rods and hockey sticks" (n.p.), reportedly mistaking him for a supporter of the right-wing strike. Das's murder was captured by reporters and broadcast on live television (Moneruzzaman and Kazi Nasir 2020).

Disclosure statement

No potential conflict of interest was reported by the author(s).

ORCID

Kathryn Hummel http://orcid.org/0000-0002-4086-4503

References

Ahmed, Sara, Claudia Castañeda, Anne-Marie Fortier, and Mimi Sheller, eds. 2003. *Uprootings/ Regroundings: Questions of Home and Migration.* Oxford: Berg.

Akhter, Maswood. 2017. "Portrayal of a Dystopic Dhaka: On Diasporic Fictional Reproduction of Bangladeshi Urbanity." In *Postcolonial Urban Outcasts: City Margins in South Asian Literature*, edited by Umme Al, edited by Umme AlWazedi and Madhurima Chakraborty, 149–165. London and New York: Routledge.

Anam, Tahmima. 2008. *A Golden Age: A Novel.* New York: HarperCollins.

Bhabha, Homi K. 1985. "Signs Taken for Wonders: Questions of Ambivalence and Authority under a Tree outside Delhi, May 1817." *Critical Inquiry* 12 (1): 144–165. doi:10.1086/448325.

Brah, Avtar. 1996. *Cartographies of Diaspora: Contesting Identities.* London: Routledge.

Chakravarty, Radha. 2008. "A Life-Sentence. Review of *Collected Poems 1996–2006*, by Kaiser Haq." *The Book Review Literary Trust* 32 (8): 2. https://www.thebookreviewindia.org/a-life-sentence/

Cheung, K-K. 2012. "The Chinese American Writer as Migrant: Ha Jin's Restive Manifesto." *Amerasia Journal* 38 (2): 2–12. doi:10.17953/amer.38.2.53q831g24kq2q231.

Choudhury, Kafeel Ahmed. 2013. "Subaltern Speaks: A Theoretical Analysis of Kaiser Haq's 'Ode on the Lungi'." *Journal of Higher Education and Research Society* 1 (1): 61–66.

Clifford, James. 1983. "On Ethnographic Authority." *Representations* 2 (Spring): 118–146. doi:10. 2307/2928386.

Conquergood, Dwight. 1991. "Rethinking Ethnography: Towards a Critical Cultural Politics." *Communication Monographs* 58 (2): 179–194. doi:10.1080/03637759109376222.

Daniel, Celia A. 1989. "The Poet as Anthropologist." In *Literature and Anthropology*, edited by W. M. Aycock and P.A. Dennis, 181–192. Lubbock: Texas Tech University Press.

Ellingson, Laura L. 2009. *Engaging Crystallization in Qualitative Research: An Introduction.* Thousand Oaks: Sage.

Featherstone, Scott, and Mike Lash, eds. 1999. *Spaces of Culture: City, Nation, World.* London: Sage.

Foucault, Michel. 1972. *The Archaeology of Knowledge.* Translated by A.M.S. Smith. New York: Pantheon Books.

Geertz, Clifford. 1988. *Works and Lives: The Anthropologist as Author.* Cambridge: Polity.

Ghosh, P S. 1993. "Bangladesh at the Crossroads: Religion and Politics." *Asian Survey* 33 (7): 697–710. doi:10.2307/2645357.

Hage, Ghassan. 2017. "Diaspora and Migration." In *A Companion to Critical and Cultural Theory*, edited by I. Szeman, S. Blacker and J. Sully, pp. 191–204. Hoboken: John Wiley & Sons.

Hajjaj, Bobby. 2020. "Nationalism and National Identity Formation in Bangladesh: A Colonial Legacy behind the Clash of Language and Religion." *Asian Journal of Comparative Politics* 20 (10): 1–14.

Haq, Kaiser. 2007a. "[Ahmede Husain] in Conversation with Kaiser Haq." *The Daily Star*, April 28. http://archive.thedailystar.net/2007/04/28/d704282101127.htm

Haq, Kaiser. 2007b. "Ode on the Lungi." *The Daily Star*, September 1. https://www.thedailystar.net/news-detail-2081

Haq, Kaiser. 2007c. *Published in the Streets of Dhaka: Collected Poems, 1966–2006.* Dhaka: University Press.

Haq, Kaiser. 2008. "[Kathryn Hummel] in Conversation with Bangladeshi Poet, Kaiser Haq." *PopMatters*, January 1. https://www.popmatters.com/in-conversation-with-bangladeshi-poet-kaiser-haq-2496189165.html

Haq, Kaiser. 2016. "Poem by Kaiser Haq in Response to Shakespeare's Sonnet 66." *British Council Literature Blog*, June 2. https://literature.britishcouncil.org/blog/tag/sonnets

Haq, Kaiser. 2017. *Pariah and Other Poems.* 2nd ed. Dhaka: Bengal Lights.

Haq, Kaiser. 2018. "An Unwitting Pariah: Kathryn Hummel in Conversation with Kaiser Haq." *Cordite Poetry Review*, August 1. http://cordite.org.au/interviews/hummel-haq/

Haq, Kaiser. 2021. "A Highbrow 'Hijra': Kaiser Haq in Conversation with Mohammad A. Quayum." In *Creative Lives: Interviews with Contemporary South Asian Diaspora Writers*, edited by Chandani Lokuge and Chris Ringrose, 136–153. Stuttgart: ibidem-Verlag.

Haq, Kaiser. n.d. "Two Poems." *The Critical Muslim*. Accessed 1 August 2021. https://www.criticalmuslim.io/two-poems-3/

Iyer, Pico. 1988. "*Video Night in Kathmandu: And Other Reports from the Not-So-FarEast*." New York: Knopf.

Jin, Ha. 2008. *The Writer as Migrant*. Chicago: University of Chicago Press.

Kamrani, Farukh. 2017. "Fall of Dhaka: How Mukti Bahini 'Cleansed' Santahar Town of Non-Bengalis." *The Express Tribune*, December 16. https://tribune.com.pk/story/1585095/mukti-bahini-cleansed-santahar-non-bengalis

Khan, Adib. 1994. *Seasonal Adjustments*. St. Leonards, NSW: Allen and Unwin.

Khan, Mohammad Jamil. 2017. "Biswajit Murder: Some Fugitives 'Seen in Public'." *The Daily Star*, December 9. https://www.thedailystar.net/backpage/biswajit-murder-some-fugitives-seen-public-1502461

Lee, Yoon Sun. 2015. "The Postcolonial Novel and Diaspora." In *The Cambridge Companion to the Postcolonial Novel*, edited by Ato Quayson, 133–151. Cambridge: Cambridge University Press.

Mand, Kanwal. 2010. "'I've Got Two Houses. One in Bangladesh and One in London ... Everybody Has': Home, Locality and Belonging(s)." *Childhood* 17 (2): 273–287. doi:10.1177/0907568210365754.

Mardorossian, C M. 2002. "From Literature of Exile to Migrant Literature." *Modern Language Studies* 32 (2): 15–33. doi:10.2307/3252040.

Mercer, Kobena. 1992. "Back to My Routes: A Postscript to the 80s." *Ten 8* 2 (3): 33–34.

Mohua, Mafruha. 2020. "Bangladesh." *The Journal of Commonwealth Literature* 55 (4): 527–537. doi:10.1177/0021989420962763.

Moneruzzaman, M, and MB Kazi Nasir. 2020. "No Justice Yet." *New Age*, September 9. https://www.newagebd.net/article/115829/no-justice-yet

Riaz, Ali 2009. "Interactions of 'Transnational' and 'Local' Islam in Bangladesh". In *Transnational Islam in South and South-East Asia: Movements, Networks and Conflict Dynamics, Edited by the National Bureau of Asian Research*. 79–100. Seattle, WA:National Bureau of Asian Research.

Said, Edward W. [1978] 2003. *Orientalism*. London: Penguin.

Said, Edward W. 2012. *Reflections on Exile*. London: Granta Books.

Seyhan, Azade. 2000. *Writing outside the Nation*. Princeton, NJ: Princeton University Press.

Spivak, Gayatri Chakravorty, and Sarah Harasym. 1990. *The Post-Colonial Critic: Interviews, Strategies, Dialogues*. New York: Routledge.

Suleri, Sara. 1992. "Woman Skin Deep: Feminism and the Postcolonial Condition." *Critical Inquiry* 18 (4): 756–769. doi:10.1086/448655.

Van Maanen, John. 1988. *Tales of the Field: On Writing Ethnography*. Chicago: University of Chicago Press.

Walkowitz, R L. 2006. "The Location of Literature: The Transnational Book and the Migrant Writer." *Contemporary Literature* 47 (4): 527–545. doi:10.1353/cli.2007.0019.

Zecchini, Laetitia. 2017. "Postcolonial South Asian Poetry." In *The Cambridge Companion to Postcolonial Poetry*, edited by Jahan Ramazani, 45–57. Cambridge: Cambridge University Press.

Toxic grace? Tahmima Anam's *The Bones of Grace* and the pollution trade

Md. Alamgir Hossain

ABSTRACT

This article explores how Tahmima Anam's 2016 novel *The Bones of Grace* responds to the notion of development as understood with reference to the transfer of pollution from rich to poor countries in an age of neo-liberal globalization. It argues that by bringing together the past experiences of environmental subalterns, their deplorable present, and macabre future, Anam constructs temporal relationality that resists the tendency of the western discourse on the pollution trade to naturalize the cumulative economic effects of neocolonial power in developing countries. While this discourse creates a singular reality around economic growth by carefully concealing the concomitant risks, Anam, by invoking different political, cultural, historical, and ecological associations, invests each aspect of reality with multiple meanings. She thus creates plural and complex realities around inequity, injustice, and poverty resulting from the pollution trade and enables the reader to see beyond mere economic growth brought about by such trade.

Economic development and the transnational trade of toxic wastes

South Asia, being one of the most ecologically vulnerable regions in the world, has witnessed a proliferation of environmental fiction in the 21st century. Among the South Asian writers who have creatively engaged with the questions of colonialism/neo-colonialism and ecological crises, Amitav Ghosh stands out. However, his non-fiction *The Great Derangement: Climate Change and the Unthinkable* (Ghosh 2016) and novels *The Hungry Tide* (Ghosh 2004) and *Gun Island* (Ghosh 2019) primarily address the issues of climate change and the Anthropocene. But, as Lawrence Buell (2017) points out, one of the risks of treating climate change as "*the* defining environmental crisis" is to "reduc[e] the others to satellite status" (89; original emphasis). It would be a mistake to assume that Ghosh does not address other environmental issues, but his concern for climate change overshadows the others.

Tahmima Anam (2016), in her novel *The Bones of Grace*, addresses the environmental crises of "satellite status" such as local food shortages, environmental degradation caused by the ship-breaking industry, and the contamination of drinking water brought about by the global demand for shrimp. Some other South Asian novelists such as Mohsin Hamid, Aravind Adiga, and Anis Shivani also grapple with different types of environmental pollution, water crisis, and resource extraction caused by urbanization and neo-liberal capitalism, but Anam intervenes in this growing body of postcolonial environmental writing in South Asia by temporally engaging with subtle forms of pollution trades, the dynamics of such trades, and their consequences that very often are obfuscated by the logic of capitalist development. In *Slow Violence and the Environmentalism of the Poor*, Rob Nixon (2011) calls for a political, imaginative, and theoretical engagement with "a violence that is neither spectacular nor instantaneous, but rather incremental and accretive" (2). Anam responds to this call by imaginatively engaging with such violence brought about by the pollution trade. Her foregrounding of the "satellite status" crises in *The Bones of Grace* warns against reducing environmental concerns to climate change and calls attention to the diverse local environmental challenges that emerge as the by-product of the transnational pollution trade in the Global South.

The efforts to attain economic development through the modernization of the globe have generated and still produce an alarming amount of industrial, chemical, medical, and radioactive wastes all around the world. Although the industrialized nations are the major producers of these wastes, they have managed to dump their wastes in the under-developed parts of the world. This transformation of some parts of the globe into dumping sites is made possible by "the power differential continuously reproduced by the stark inequality of 'development' and" (Bauman 2004, 6). Economically and technologically advanced nations, in the name of assisting poor countries to develop their economic conditions, introduce strategies to dispose of their wastes by transferring them to low-income countries. The logic of economic development via exporting "dirty industries" (Summers 1991, n.p.) to poor countries obfuscates the unequal power relations governing modern trade practices and "leaves unexamined the cumulative economic effects of colonial power, that is, of the still-working mechanisms of dispossession, displacement, and death that facilitate the expropriation of the productive capacity of the lands and bodies of the 'others of Europe' and" (da Silva 2015, 35).

The present article examines how Anam's (2016) *The Bones of Grace* challenges the tendency of such logic to obscure the attendant effects of the pollution trade and its asymmetrical power relations, by looking at economic development from a temporal perspective. I contend that Anam, by using analepsis, prolepsis, and allusions, constructs temporal relationality that situates the pollution trade and its effects within larger social, political, economic, and ecological contexts and thus resists the tendency of the western discourse on the pollution trade to naturalize the "cumulative economic effects" of neocolonial power in developing countries. By "temporal relationality", I mean temporal awareness that perceives events and actions as taking place not merely at a specific point of time but in relation to time: to past, present, and future. This perception of events and actions within a broader temporal framework enables one to see beyond the immediate economic benefits arising from the transnational trade of toxic wastes.

The Bones of Grace, the final volume of Anam's Bengal trilogy, recounts its protagonist's struggle to negotiate her roles as an obedient daughter and a wife on the one hand and a passionate lover on the other.[1] Zubaida Haque is the adopted daughter of a wealthy Bangladeshi family in Dhaka, who falls in love with an American man, Elijah Strong, while studying at Harvard. Zubaida's love for Elijah, despite her commitment to marry her childhood friend Rashid in Bangladesh, puts her in a critical situation, which adds to the already existing ontological crisis caused by her awareness of being an adopted child. Her situation is aggravated when she encounters violence in Pakistan while working as a palaeontologist. On her return from Pakistan to Bangladesh, following her parents' wishes, Zubaida marries Rashid, and later suffers a miscarriage. To overcome her trauma, she goes to Chittagong where she meets ship-breakers, acts as an interpreter for a non-governmental organization (NGO), and becomes aware of the devastating effects of global capitalism on the human and the natural environment in the Global South. Her acquaintance with Anwar – her sister's former lover – in Chittagong unravels the mystery of her birth and puts an end to her quest for identity. Zubaida's experience in the ship-breaking yard and her encounter with Anwar profoundly impact her inner self and shape her later course of action. By depicting Zubaida as an interpreter who helps the ship-breakers, and Gabriela, a British researcher, communicate with each other, Anam gives voice to the environmental subalterns. These subalterns tell Gabriela individual and collective stories of suffering at home and in the ship-breaking yard, for documentary purposes. In addition to depicting Zubaida's personal crises, the novel represents the ship-breakers' miserable reduction to bare life by the forces of capitalism, demonstrating the exploitation of labour and the environment caused by the ideology of capitalism.

Critics and reviewers of *The Bones of Grace* primarily focus on the issues of love, identity, and the narrator's split self in their analysis. In her review, Arifa Akbar (2016) identifies "the shattering effects of conflicted love", "questions around family and belonging", and "fractures in identity", as the "powerful element[s]" (n.p.) in the text. While Amy Brady (2016) calls *The Bones of Grace* "a tale of self-discovery" (n.p.), Philip Marchand (2016) discovers "an approach related to romance" (n.p.) in the novel. But the novel is not only about its narrator's internal crisis, romance, and identity; it also explores the machinery of neo-liberal capitalism – the political and economic practices that aim at safeguarding capitalist interest by facilitating the flow of capital and transferring the control of economic forces from the public to the private sector – and its effects on the people and ecology of Bangladesh. The emphasis on Zubaida's predicament overlooks the novel's representation of the social, economic, and environmental catastrophe caused by different forms of pollution trades such as ship-breaking and shrimp farming. Even the single study of Anam's portrayal of the ship-breaking industry in Bangladesh, Arthur Rose's (2018) "In the Wake of Asbestos: Ship-Building and Ship-Breaking in Ross Raisin's *Waterline* and Tahmima Anam's *The Bones of Grace*", has this limitation. Although Rose examines the risks of working in the hazardous environment of the ship-breaking yard as represented in *The Bones of Grace*, the dispossession, displacement, and exploitation resulting from the ship-breaking industry remains outside the scope of his analysis. But Anam, in addition to depicting the danger of working in the ship-breaking yard, also traces how pollution trades through globalization gradually exhaust the productivity of the poor and the environment and eventually turn them into disposable entities. Consequently, Anam's engagement with ship-breaking and shrimp farming (also unexplored in current scholarship), forms of the pollution trade that strive for economic development at the cost of life and the environment, requires critical examination. In the present article, I analyse the ways Anam deploys temporality to complicate the taken-for-granted outcome of the pollution trade in her novel.

The notion of economic development via pollution trades, because of its capitalist nature, primarily focuses on the present. In the capitalist project, "profit and the [...] exact use of time are linked together" (Thrift 1996, 172). This capitalist relationship between profit and time can be expressed by the dictum, as E.P. Thompson (1967) puts it bluntly, that "time is money" (86). Since the past cannot generate capitalist profit and the future is not yet available, the logic of pollution trades seeks to exploit the present. Because of its presentist attitude, the notion of development via pollution trades ignores the broader context of time. But Anam, in order to draw temporal and causal connections between the past and the present, has her characters recount their environmental and economic experiences of the past in relation to their present. To point to the future consequences of the neo-liberal development project, at times she juxtaposes two situations – food shortage and shrimp farming – and at other times makes her primary narrator Zubaida predict the ship-breakers' impending doom. Thus, Anam brings together the past experiences of environmental subalterns, their deplorable present, and macabre future, creating what Seymour Chatman (1990) calls internal "chrono-logic" (9) to challenge the temporal basis on which the logic of the pollution trade rests.[2]

Articles or reports also challenge the logic of the pollution trade by providing data and statistics but are "incapable of representing individual experiences of catastrophe, and of simulating the experiences of subjects whose lives and livelihoods are [...] shaped by [the pollution trade]" (Poray-Wybranowska 2021, 14). Anam's novel, on the other hand, by using the first-person point of view, represents the individual and collective experiences of the victims of this trade, and their struggle to cope with its damaging consequences. Another South Asian novel that deserves mention is Indra Sinha's (2007) *Animal's People*. The novel's first-person narrator, Animal, recounts his traumatic experiences and that of other victims of the Bhopal gas disaster, both during and after 20 years of the event, demonstrating their physical, psychological, economic, and environmental dispossession brought about by the hazardous industry's economically motivated transnational relocation. This type of literary engagement with economic development and environmental degradation invites readers to engage with questions of development and the environment in a compelling way. However, while Sinha explicitly depicts the consequences of the disaster, Anam hypothetically projects the possible outcomes of the pollution trade and thus pushes the reader's imagination further to grapple with its complexity. For this reason, *The Bones of Grace* demands special attention from both readers and critics.

Neo-liberal capitalism and the emergence of the ship-breaking industry in Bangladesh

In *The Bones of Grace*, Anam represents the struggles of the poor to survive both ecological and man-made crises caused by the uncontrolled flow and accumulation of capital embodied in Bangladesh's ship-breaking industry. Despite encountering infernal working conditions and environmental hazards, the ship-breakers have no choice but to work in order to survive and support their families. Anam combines stories of the workers from the north, their experience in the southeast, and the origin story of ship-breaking in Bangladesh to suggest that the workers' predicament stems from the adoption of an unregulated neo-liberal policy aimed at achieving economic development.

After going over some documents at the Shipsafe office, Zubaida learns about the beginning of ship-breaking in Chittagong. Referring to the genesis of this industry, she states that

> there were apocryphal stories about how it had all started – a cyclone in the Bay of Bengal, a ship banked on the shore, a group of scavengers, the discovery of steel and then, eventually, businessmen who turned ill fortune into profit. (Anam 2016, 142)

This origin story recalls the country's history of resorting to structural adjustment programmes. Initially, after independence in 1971, Bangladesh adopted a state-socialist economic approach, but as Fahimul Quadir (2000, 200) observes, under the increasing pressure of the World Bank and the International Monetary Fund (IMF), the country eschewed this approach and started liberalizing its economy in the late 1970s. The emergence of the ship-breaking industry is a consequence of this liberalization. Although the first ship-breaking in Chittagong occurred as the result of an accident in the 1960s, it was not until 1974, when the Karnafuli Metal Works Ltd bought a damaged ship as scrap, that commercial ship-breaking in Bangladesh began (Hossain and Islam 2006, 5). The country's economic liberalization, along with the developed nations' intentions "to get rid of [their ship-breaking] industry" because of environmental concerns, provided "Bangladeshi industrialists [... with an] opportunit[y] [...] [for] huge profit" (5), and facilitated the proliferation of the ship-breaking industry in the 1980s. In *The Bones of Grace*, Anam situates this industry in relation to historical events, local and global capitalism, environmental degradation, and exploitation of labour with a view to problematizing the role of this seemingly profit-generating industry in the development of Bangladesh. Her allusion to the origin of the ship-breaking industry in Bangladesh further draws attention to the unequal power relations that cause developing countries to liberalize their economies to receive financial aid.

Anam's historicizing of the origin of the ship-breaking industry in Bangladesh sheds light on its nature, operation and evolution. For Zubaida, as Rose (2018) observes, this origin story "evokes a history of capitalist expansion from the chance conditions of a natural event" (150–151). Although Zubaida understands the turning of "ill fortune into profit" as taking place at a specific time in the past, Anam's perception of this conversion is not limited to a particular period of time; rather, her portrayal of the ship-breakers in Chittagong shows the perpetuation of this transformation through to later decades. The first ship-breaking in the country might have resulted from a ship-owner's ill-fortune as the result of a cyclone, but later on, with the availability of cheap labour and market, the victims changed. As Md. M. Maruf Hossain and Mohammad Mahmudul Islam (2006) point out, because of the availability of cheap labour and lack of strict environmental laws in Bangladesh, from the early 1980s the ship-owners from industrialized countries started sending their vessels to Bangladesh to maximize their profits (2–6). The foreign ship-owners, along with local businessmen, become profiteers. Anam's novel delineates how, in the changed scenario, the workers of the ship-breaking yard, whose labour the capitalists employ, endure ill fortune brought about by other types of natural calamity and land dispossession.

Environmental crises, exploitation of labour, dispossession of land, and the ship-breaking industry

Most of the workers in the pullers category (who remove broken parts of the demolished ship from the beach) in the novel come from the northern part of the country and are victims of Monga, a "seasonal food insecurity in ecologically vulnerable and economically weak parts of Northwestern Bangladesh" (Sarker, Mian, and Roy 2012, 108). During their interview sessions with Zubaida and Gabriela, the pullers of Prosperity Ship-breaking recount poignant stories of their departure from the north and migration to the southeast to join the ship-breaking in Sitakunda. Belal, a worker in Prosperity Ship-breaking, describes the circumstances under which he left home seven years ago because of Monga. The narrator writes:

> [Belal] thought [they] had enough rice. It was [his] mother and [his] father, [his] wife, three children, another coming. […]. It was two months before the harvest that the rice ran out. He went to sell his labour, but there was no work going. His father walked into the fields one day and didn't come back. But still there wasn't enough. He had a daughter, three years old, and she was the first to go. Then winter set in, and, with it, a fever that spread through the village. […] Now he works to feed the two remaining children, left up north with his brother. (Anam 2016, 171)

Monga itself is not a natural disaster, but a consequence of other natural calamities, such as "floods […] river erosion, drought, hailstorms, excessive rainfall, severe cold, cyclones, [and] water surges [caused by] climate change" (Mazumder and Wencong 2012, 364). Hence, Monga-affected people are the indirect victims of natural disasters. Workers in the novel like Russel and Belal, finding no other alternative, join the ship-breaking industry to survive and support their family in the north. The capitalist owners of the ship-breaking enterprises exploit the labour of these victims, profiting by their misfortune. A glimpse into the past of the northern ship-breakers makes one aware of the complex relationship between environmental crises, the struggle for survival, pollution trades, and capitalist exploitation.

On the one hand, ship-breaking exploits the labour of the Monga-affected dispossessed people from the north; on the other, it contributes to the dispossession of land in Sitakunda and the surrounding area. Zubaida mentions that, unlike the people from the north, who have no alternative to working in the ship-breaking yard, the local people in Sitakunda join ship-breaking "in exchange for permission to use their land" (Anam 2016, 168). Anam does not explain why the locals would want to exchange their agricultural land for permission to work in the ship-breaking industry, but analysis of the event in relation to the pollution trade provides some clues. Hossain and Islam (2006) point out that during ship-breaking, "oil residues and the other refuses are […] spilled and mixed with soil and water in the beach" (25), which results in the contamination of soil with toxic elements in the coastal area in Chittagong. This may have caused difficulties for farmers in cultivating their land, leading them to barter it for work at the ship-breaking yard. The exchange, or rather the dispossession of land, disturbs the ecological balance in the coastal area of Chittagong by reducing the amount of agricultural land. The narrative of economic development disregards or rather hides these other forms of reality involving dispossession, environmental degradation, social power dynamics, and economic gains because it prioritizes economic growth. Anam's focus on the experiences of the workers, however, illustrates the other side of economic development.

The impact of ship-breaking on human life and the environment

Since ship demolition generates a number of substances such as lead, cadmium, arsenic, zinc, etc. that are defined as hazardous wastes under the Basel Convention, ship-breaking is recognized as a hazardous industry. These hazards "fall into two categories: intoxication by dangerous substances, and accidents on the plots" (Hossain and Islam 2006, 12). Anam attends to both categories in her representations. The immediate victims of the hazards are the workers who risk their lives to dismantle the ship. Zubaida evokes this lethal environment when she describes the smelting of the scrap derived from the demolition of an oil tanker: "On the shoreline, the smelter was going at full speed, and the air was thick with the astringent smell of burning metal" (Anam 2016, 141). She also reflects on the surroundings in which the pullers tried to carry a propeller to a truck: "[e]verything smelled of the chemicals thrown up by the ships and the burn of the metal as it was processed, but their faces bore no trace of disgust, no recognition that the very air they breathed was poison" (161–162). Rose (2018) attributes the workers' failure to recognize the danger of the toxic environment to their concern about injuries in the workplace (141–142). Although they are not conscious of damaging effects of their toxic environment, Anam points out "latent morbidities, [...] conditions that are most risky for the characters, irrespective of whatever actually does or does not kill them" (141), created by the ship-breaking industry in Chittagong. The narrator emphasizes the real danger of dealing with toxic materials by identifying the presence of harmful chemicals in the blood of workers of Prosperity Ship-breaking. While looking for Mo, the child worker in Prosperity Ship-breaking, Anwar, a ship-breaker in search of his beloved and daughter in Sitakunda, encounters workers with "arsenic and all kinds of shit in their veins and all over their skin" (Anam 2016, 250). He also comments that "every day I fall to sleep with poison in my blood" (237). Anam does not elaborate on the consequences of these toxic substances experienced by the ship-breakers,[3] but these references to workers intoxicated by chemicals point to the medical and environmental crisis caused by the industry.

Although Anam does not depict any death arising from the contaminated environment, she explicitly refers to what Nixon (2011) calls "slow violence"; that is, "a violence that occurs gradually and out of sight, a violence of delayed destruction that is dispersed across time and space, an attritional violence that is typically not viewed as violence at all" (2). Zubaida's description of the ship-breakers' living arrangements shows how the greedy owners of the industry gradually push the workers towards death. She observes: "the men in the neighboring beaches didn't get anything, they just lived on whatever ship they were breaking, which was bad news, because if the fires didn't kill you, the fumes from the tanks would finish you off slowly" (Anam 2016, 168). The workers are victims of both risky working conditions and environmental pollution; a ship-breaker who succeeds in escaping one will fall victim to the other. Anam's projection of the Chittagong ship-breaking industry as destroying lives of ship-breakers by inflicting immediate and slow violence necessitates rethinking the issue of development through the transnational shipment of hazardous substances.

In *Wasted Lives: Modernity and its Outcasts*, Zygmunt Bauman (2004) argues that "human waste [...] is an inescapable side-effect of [...] *economic progress*" (5; original emphasis) brought about by modernization. For Bauman, "the modernizing niches of the globe" turned the so-called "backward" and "underdeveloped" parts of the world into "ready-made dumping sites for the human waste of modernization" (5–6). Here the term "human waste" refers to humans who are seen as excess, superfluous, no longer of use to society. In *The Bones of Grace*, Anam extends Bauman's argument and suggests that the quest for economic progress through the pollution trade transforms some parts of the globe into dumping grounds not only for human waste, but also for the toxic waste of the developed nations. She condemns such spatial racialization by depicting the morbid surroundings that stretch beyond the ship-breaking yard and predicting the fatal consequences of the waste dumped in the racialized parts of the world.

The pollution caused by the ship-breaking industry does not remain confined to the ship-breaking yard but contaminates the neighbouring areas as well. Broken and unusable items of a dismantled ship find their way from the ship-breaking yard to the surrounding scrapyard where no regulatory framework exists to manage the hazardous materials appropriately. On her way from Chittagong to the Shipsafe office at Sitakunda, Zubaida sees "vast scrapyards of things that looked like they'd been rescued from a warzone: broken refrigerators, oxygen tanks, rows and rows of lifebuoys, toilet bowls, washing machines, [...] compressors" (136). Anam's protagonist visualizes the impact of this waste in terms of a disastrous future: "how bizarre it all looked, like a glimpse into an apocalyptic future where everything was salvaged and half-broken" (136). Zubaida connects the scrapyards to her own sense of loss and destruction, remarking: "the sight of [the scrapyards ...] matched the chaos I felt within me" (136). She is haunted by thoughts of her biological parents whom she has never seen. Moreover, she has recently suffered a miscarriage. By comparing the disordered state of the scrapyards to the narrator's internal chaos, Anam metaphorically implies the possible disaster resulting from the hazardous waste of the industrialized nations; the analogy suggests that human trauma arising from an external disaster can also reflect it, creating a more immediate impact.

Pollution trades and shrimp farming

While examining the modus operandi of the pollution trade, Anam points to the predicament of poor countries such as Bangladesh that, in order to attain economic development, naively fall victim to such trade. Developed countries, taking advantage of neo-liberal globalization, manipulate the trade in such a way that poor countries, whether importing or exporting, always remain repositories for toxic waste. While ship-breaking demonstrates that developed nations dump hazardous substances into poor countries, Anam introduces shrimp farming to show the Global North's import from the Global South and the consequent generation of toxic waste there. On the one hand, developed nations export their toxic wastes in the form of decommissioned ships to Bangladesh, creating human and environmental hazards; on the other, by importing shrimp, they also put locals at risk of serious ecological damage. Thus, in both export and import the Global North enjoys a cleaner environment, better life, and greater luxury at the cost of toxification and environmental degradation in the Global South.

In *Postcolonial Ecologies: Literatures of the Environment*, Elizabeth DeLoughrey and George B. Handley (2011) observe that "resource extraction initiatives like deforestation, mining, and the liberalization of internal markets have all radically altered the postcolonial environment" (16). In *The Bones of Grace*, Anam (2016) depicts how the global demand for shrimp contributes to the depletion of coastal resources and "radically alter[s]" the local environment. Because of the great demand for shrimp around the world and the potential for profit, many farmers in the southwestern coastal region of Bangladesh engage in shrimp farming instead of cultivating crops, vegetables, or fruit. Since, as Anwar's fellow traveller affirms, there is a "lot of money in shrimp" (2016, 198), to augment their profit, "large-scale commercial farmers coerce [...] smallholders [...] to convert their freshwater fields into shrimp farms" (Lovatt 2016, n.p.). Anam depicts the effects of this conversion by registering Anwar's experience on his way from Khulna to Chittagong.

After returning from Dubai, Anwar sets out to find his former beloved, Megna, whom he abandoned earlier when leaving to work in Dubai. When travelling by bus, he is puzzled on seeing through the window a scene that he cannot reconcile with his past experience, and he asks his fellow passenger:

> On the road either side of me, all the paddy fields are flooded. Why, I ask the boy sitting next to me on the bus. [...] I haven't seen winter rice for ten years, but I know what it looks like, yellow and brown and green. And it's dry by now, January when it's cold and there's no rain. "That's not rice," the boy says, with a big sag of his shoulder. "It's shrimp."
>
> I look closer. The water's dark. I try to smell it. The little worms are crawling around in there like a giant itch. (Anam 2016, 198)

Shrimp farms have replaced paddy fields; the poor local farmers, instead of growing food for themselves, now produce a delicacy for rich countries. Jason Cons and Kasia Paprocki (2014) trace this trend of shrimp farming at the cost of local agriculture back to the structural adjustment policies in the 1980s. They observe that "since the Bangladesh government began developing the aquaculture export market in the 1980s - under direction from IMF - and World Bank-imposed structural adjustment policies - this [southwestern coastal] region has been inundated with shrimp" (n.p.). What motivates the farmers to discard their age-old agricultural practices and to cultivate shrimp instead is the lure of monetary profit gained through the export of shrimp. From this perspective, the conversion of paddy fields into shrimp farms could be considered as the dispossession of cultivable land brought about by the neo-liberal mechanisms of global trade. Like ship-breaking, the shrimp industry also exploits the labour of those whom it has dispossessed. By juxtaposing Anwar's memory of earlier agricultural practices with the current practice of shrimp farming, Anam depicts the reality of dispossession brought about by the quest for economic development and neo-liberal forces.

The takeover of traditional agricultural land by the shrimp industry has deleterious effects on the local ecology. Cons and Paprocki (2014) remark that "the massive adoption of shrimp aquaculture has laid waste to ecologically sensitive zones - contributing to the destruction of coastal mangrove forests; the loss of local biodiversity; and rampant pollution through the discharge of shrimp pond effluents into local ecosystems" (n.p.). Because of excessive shrimp farming, "salinity seeps ever further inland" (Lovatt 2016, n. p.) and contaminates freshwater. Anam represents the water pollution resulting from the shrimp industry by recording the experience of Anwar's wife, Shathi, and that of his fellow bus passengers: "I [Anwar] ask a few other people about the shrimp. They say the water's gone salty because the shrimp like it that way. I wonder if that's why Shathi's been complaining about the water in our well" (2016, 198). By referring to the cultivation of export-oriented shrimp and its harmful impact on the ecology of southwestern Bangladesh, Anam invites the reader to re-evaluate their understanding of the pollution trade. On the face of it, the export of shrimp is an innocuous transnational trade that does not involve any transboundary shipment of hazardous waste, but its impact on the local ecology suggests that, though, seemingly harmless, it contributes to environmental pollution in the Global South. Neo-liberal globalization has expanded the dimension of the pollution trade, and Anam offers an insight into the subtle encroachment of these trades with the lure of money, the transformation of paddy fields into shrimp farms, and the contamination of water.

The myth of economic development and its reality

Proponents of the pollution trade might argue that despite its damaging effects on the environment, the trade contributes to the development of the country by generating employment opportunities for poor people. Anam does not counter this potential for creating opportunity, but in situating them in relation to development, capitalism, and workers' well-being, she points to the social crises, such as inequality and uneven development, which they catalyse. While commenting on economic development at the periphery of the world system (regions other than Europe, North America, and Japan), Amin (1974) argues that its basis consists of production for export and consumption of luxury goods (12–14). The "export sector", Amin observes, is created

> under an impulse from the centre [... with a view to] obtaining from the periphery products which are the basic elements of constant capital (raw material) or of variable capital (food products) at production costs lower than those at the centre for similar products. (12–13)

The export sector, by supplying cheap labour and both constant and variable capital to the centre, causes unequal development in the periphery instead of contributing to its real development. The export-oriented shrimp industry in Bangladesh represents "the shaping of the periphery to the requirements of the centre" (13) at the cost of the margin's own needs. The shrimp industry offers employment as revealed in the conversation between Anwar and his fellow traveller, who works in a shrimp farm and wants to talk to his boss about giving Anwar a job, but it limits the production of food for the local population. The potential result is a scarcity of food that can only be mitigated by importing food, possibly at high rates. The food crisis might also cause large-scale migration within the country. In the novel, the Monga-affected northern region and its people serve as a forewarning of the economic and ecological disaster that could result from the export-oriented shrimp industry in the south. The need to import food at a high rate or the migration of people can easily offset any so-called development that the export of shrimp might achieve.

Like the shrimp industry, the ship-breaking industry also offers employment opportunities to people from both the north and the south, and provides much-needed steel to the country, but by juxtaposing the national demand for steel with the conditions of the workers who produce it, Anam questions the concept of development represented by the demand for steel for construction purposes. When Zubaida first meets Mirza Ali, the manager of Prosperity Ship-breaking, he "reel[s] off statistics of how many tons of steel his yard had sold to the construction industry" (Anam 2016, 142–143). On another occasion, Ali remarks that "ship-breaking is important for Bangladesh. We need steel. Lot[s] of construction everywhere" (149). Lots of construction and the flourishing of the construction industry suggest material development in the country, which can be measured by indices such as the gross domestic product (GDP) and gross national product (GNP), but this type of material development does not consider human well-being or environmental sustainability. While construction work enables the building of big residential or commercial complexes, the ship-breakers lack a safe and hygienic place in which to live or work. In contrast to the material development embodied in Sally's "over-air-conditioned apartment" (81) with "leather dining chairs [... and a] white baby grand against the sliding doors" (80), and "big houses behind high gates" (81) in Gulshan neighbourhood, are "shacks behind the [ship]yard" where the ship-breakers live crammed together in exchange for "about half [their] pay" (237). The sheer contrast between the flourishing of the construction and steel industries that thrive on the labour of the ship-breakers, and the wretched conditions of the ship-breakers themselves suggests that the ship-breaking industry, instead of contributing to the country's improvement, causes uneven development by exploiting the workers' cheap labour.

In addition to human exploitation, the ship-breaking industry also exploits the natural environment and displaces labour to create unequal social conditions in the country. Karl Marx (1976) points out that "the greater the centralization of the means of production, the greater is the corresponding concentration of workers within a given space" (811–812). In Chittagong, the availability of a number of means of production such as "long, flat uniform intertidal zone, [a]n extended beach with tidal difference of 6 meters, [p]rotection by the Bay of Bengal, [and] [s]table weather conditions" (Hossain and Islam 2006, 5–6) contributed to the burgeoning of ship-breaking. Since these means of production are available all year round, the industry draws a large number of workers from different parts of the country throughout the year. In the novel, the Monga-affected people from the north join ship-breaking for seasonal employment. However, Anam implies that this seasonal movement of workers created by the centralization of the means of production in the ship-breaking industry diverts attention from any possible solution to the affliction of Monga. One of its major causes is the "non-availability of working facilities at the off-farm sector" (Sarker, Mian, and Roy 2012, 110); that is, when farmers cannot work the agricultural land due to natural calamity, they remain unemployed, because only limited opportunities exist in the non-agricultural sector; hence they seek seasonal employment in the shipyard. Zubaida learns that

> the pullers came from the north of the country, where there weren't any jobs and the threat of famine hung over them every winter [...]. [T]hese men [...] were recruited in the winter, paid by the hour, and sent home at the end of the season, their pockets only a little fuller than when they arrived. (Anam 2016, 168)

The easy availability of seasonal employment in the shipyard distracts the farmers from seeking permanent solutions to their problem by developing alternative sources of employment in the north. In other words, the past of the Monga-affected people creates their present, and vice versa. Consequently, certain parts of the north remain underdeveloped and become a constant source of labour for other parts of the country, resulting in human and geographical uneven development. As Harry Harootunian (2000) observes, capitalism, in its drive for "constant expansion", produces "permanent unevenness, permanent imbalance between various sectors of the social formations" (xv). As a result, "some areas [are ...] sacrificed for the development of others, such as the countryside for the city [...] the colony for the metropole, or even one city for another" (xv). In *The Bones of Grace*, Anam portrays how human and geographical uneven development affects those who live at the margin of the society and depend on nature for their survival.

Conclusion: Space for resistance

The victims of pollution trades in the novel are caught up in the web of global capitalism in the name of development. Anam sees potential in the efforts of the locals to resist the inroad of capitalist development projects that exploit the environment and native labour to gain economic benefits. In the novel, Rubana, an activist, along with a local NGO called Shipsafe, has been working for the protection of the local environment and the ship-breakers. Rubana "had won a few injunctions in court" in her attempts to have "a ban on the whole industry" (Anam 2016, 144), but the victory has been partial because "soon the appropriate palms were greased and the court orders were ignored and the ships began to arrive again" (144). Now Rubana's NGO works in collaboration with the British researcher Gabriela whose film *Rainbow Warrior* could provide the locals with evidence that can strengthen their case against the ship-breaking industry in the High Court. The local authority in the form of the court or the environment ministry can permit or ban ship-breaking at its own discretion, and thus can control the global pollution trade at the local level. Anam bestows agency on the native and native institutions to resist the onslaught of neo-liberal globalization that seeks to thrive by exploiting the labour and resources of the locals.

In *The Storyworld Accord: Econarratology and Postcolonial Narratives*, Erin James (2015) states that "storyworlds [...] provide readers access to highly subjective understandings of what it is like to live in, conceptualize, and experience a given space and time" (xii).[4] Anam's storyworld in her novel, created through the stories of Zubaida, Anwar, and the ship-breakers, produces the immediacy of the victims' predicament and their deplorable experiences, and thus compels readers to think about possible solutions to these problems. In *Climate Crisis and the 21st-Century British Novel*, Astrid Bracke (2018) observes that "in novels, past and present can be revisited, different futures can be imagined, and responses and experiences tried out" (7). In *The Bones of Grace*, Anam revisits the past, depicts the present, and imagines the future in order to question the capitalist notion of development via pollution trades. However, the novel is not merely an indictment of pollution trades, but also a call for action. Stories, as Kate Rigby (2015) asserts, can "shape how we prepare for, respond to, and recover from increasingly frequent and [...] frequently unfamiliar forms of eco-catastrophe" (2). Anam's novel, by representing the wretched condition of the ship-breakers, their environmental experiences, uneven material development, and the potential of the locals to resist the trade of toxic waste, invites the reader not only to prepare for and respond to different forms of eco-catastrophe resulting from the pollution trade, but also to resist the very cause of such catastrophe, namely neo-liberal capitalism.

Notes

1. Tahmima Anam's Bengal Trilogy recounts the story of three generations of the Haque family. The first two volumes of the trilogy are *A Golden Age* (2007) and *The Good Muslim* (2011). *The Bones of Grace* (2016) marks the end of the trilogy.
2. For Chatman, "chrono-logic" is a unique characteristic of narrative. By "chrono-logic", he refers to two kinds of time – external and internal – that narrative involves. He observes that "[n]arrative entails movement through time not only 'externally' (the duration of the presentation of the novel, film, play) but also 'internally' (the duration of the sequence of events that constitute the plot)" (1990, 9). The internal logic of the narrative can also "evoke a certain situation or state of affairs" (9) by making events, whether closely connected or not, work together.
3. For an insightful analysis of Anam's exclusion of the effects of toxic chemicals on the ship-breakers, see Rose (2018).
4. James (2015) defines storyworld as "a mental model of context and environment within which a narrative's characters function and to which readers transport themselves as they read narratives (253).

Disclosure statement

No potential conflict of interest was reported by the author.

ORCID

Md. Alamgir Hossain http://orcid.org/0000-0003-2011-3996

References

Akbar, Arifa. 2016. "*The Bones of Grace*, by Tahmima Anam." *Financial Times*, May 20. https://www.ft.com/content/834c6eb6-1856-11e6-b197-a4af20d5575e
Amin, Samir. 1974. "Accumulation and Development: A Theoretical Model." *Review of African Political Economy* 1 (1): 9–26. doi:10.1080/03056247408703234.
Anam, Tahmima. 2016. *The Bones of Grace*. New York: HarperCollins.
Bauman, Zygmunt. 2004. *Wasted Lives: Modernity and Its Outcasts*. Oxford: Polity.
Bracke, Astrid. 2018. *Climate Crisis and the 21st-Century British Novel*. London: Bloomsbury.
Brady, Amy. 2016. "*The Bones of Grace* Pulls Back the Curtain on Bangladesh." *Chicago Review of Books*, July 6. https://chireviewofbooks.com/2016/07/06/bones-of-grace-pulls-back-the-curtain-on-bangladesh
Buell, Lawrence. 2017. "The Anthropocene Takeover: Hazards for Environmental Humanists." *English Language Notes* 55 (1–2): 89–99. doi:10.1215/00138282-55.1-2.89.
Chatman, Seymour. 1990. *Coming to Terms: The Rhetoric of Narrative in Fiction and Film*. Ithaca, NY: Cornell University Press.

Cons, Jason, and Kasia Paprocki. 2014. "Brackish Waters and Salted Lands: The Social Cost of Shrimp in Bangladesh." *Food First*. https://www.foodfirst.org/publication/brackish-waters-and-salted-lands/

da Silva, Denise Ferreira. 2015. "Globality." *Critical Ethnic Studies* 1 (1): 33–38. doi:10.5749/jcritethnstud.1.1.0033.

DeLoughrey, Elizabeth, and George B. Handley. 2011. "Introduction: Toward an Aesthetics of the Earth." In *Postcolonial Ecologies: Literatures of the Environment*, edited by Elizabeth DeLoughrey and George B. Handley, 3–39. New York: Oxford University Press.

Ghosh, Amitav. 2004. *The Hungry Tide*. Boston/New York: Houghton Mifflin Harcourt.

Ghosh, Amitav. 2016. *The Great Derangement: Climate Change and the Unthinkable*. Chicago: University of Chicago Press.

Ghosh, Amitav. 2019. *Gun Island*. New York: Farrar, Straus and Giroux.

Harootunian, Harry. 2000. *Overcome by Modernity: History, Culture, and Community in Interwar Japan*. Princeton, NJ: Princeton University Press.

Hossain, Md. M. Maruf, and Mohammad Mahmudul Islam. 2006. *Ship Breaking Activities and Its Impact on the Coastal Zone of Chittagong, Bangladesh: Towards Sustainable Management*. Chittagong: Young Power in Social Action.

James, Erin. 2015. *The Storyworld Accord: Econarratology and Postcolonial Narratives*. Lincoln and London: University of Nebraska Press.

Lovatt, Joanna. 2016. "The Bangladesh Shrimp Farmers Facing Life on the Edge." *The Guardian*, February 17. https://www.theguardian.com/global-development-professionals-network/2016/feb/17/the-bangladesh-shrimp-farmers-facing-life-on-the-edge

Marchand, Philip. 2016. "Love among the Ruins: Tahmima Anam's *the Bones of Grace* Explores Life after Ecstasy." *National Post*, June 19. https://nationalpost.com/entertainment/books/book-reviews/love-among-the-ruins-tahmima-anams-the-bones-of-grace-explores-life-after-ecstacy

Marx, Karl. 1976. *Capital: A Critique of Political Economy*. Vol. 1. Translated by Ben Fowkes. New York: Penguin Books.

Mazumder, Mohummed Shofi Ullah, and Lu Wencong. 2012. "Monga Vulnerability in the Northern Part of Bangladesh." *African Journal of Agricultural Research* 7 (3): 358–366. doi:10.5897/AJAR11.849.

Nixon, Rob. 2011. *Slow Violence and the Environmentalism of the Poor*. Cambridge, MA: Harvard University Press.

Poray-Wybranowska, Justyna. 2021. *Climate Change, Ecological Catastrophe, and the Contemporary Postcolonial Novel*. New York: Routledge.

Quadir, Fahimul. 2000. "The Political Economy of Pro-market Reforms in Bangladesh: Regime Consolidation through Economic Liberalization?" *Contemporary South Asia* 9 (2): 197–212. doi:10.1080/713658731.

Rigby, Kate. 2015. *Dancing with Disaster: Environmental Histories, Narratives, and Ethics for Perilous Times*. Charlottesville and London: University of Virginia Press.

Rose, Arthur. 2018. "In the Wake of Asbestos: Ship-building and Ship-breaking in Ross Raisin's *Waterline* and Tahmima Anam's *the Bones of Grace*." *Ariel: A Review of International English Literature* 49 (4): 139–161. doi:10.1353/ari.2018.0032.

Sarker, J.R., M.R.U. Mian, and S.S. Roy. 2012. "Farmers' Perception about Causes and Remedies of Monga in Hatibandha Upazila of Lalmonirhat District." *Journal of the Bangladesh Agricultural University* 10 (1): 107–118. doi:10.3329/jbau.v10i1.12101.

Sinha, Indra. 2007. *Animal's People*. New York: Simon & Schuster.

Summers, Lawrence. 1991. "The Bank Memo." *The Whirled Bank*. https://www.whirledbank.org/ourwords/summers.html

Thompson, E.P. 1967. "Time, Work-discipline, and Industrial Capitalism." *Past & Present* 38 (1): 56–97. doi:10.1093/past/38.1.56.

Thrift, Nigel. 1996. *Spatial Formations*. London: Sage Publications.

Beyond national(ist) binaries: The case of Zia Haider Rahman's *In the Light of What We Know*

Md Rezaul Haque

ABSTRACT

This article reads Zia Haider Rahman's debut novel *In the Light of What We Know* (2014), focusing on its interventionist trajectory with regards to Bangladeshi and Pakistani national discourse. It analyses the representational subversions this intervention entails and the factors that enable them. Rahman is a member of the Bangladeshi diaspora in Britain, and this physical distance from the home country is one factor that shapes his critical reading of the dominant rhetoric of both nationalisms. The fact that he is a second- rather than first-generation immigrant also contributes to his relationship with the mainstream Bangladeshi and Pakistani national discourse. The article argues that by intervening in the officially sanctioned national narratives of Bangladesh and Pakistan, Rahman initiates a healthy new trend in Bangladeshi diasporic literature – one which helps to build a bridge of empathy between the two nations locked in an endless cycle of antagonism and misunderstanding.

Introduction: Nationalism and fictional interventions

In the Light of What We Know, Zia Haider Rahman's (b. 1969) 2014 debut novel is an interventionist text. Its interventions can be located in a range of discursive domains, including Bengali – or more precisely Bangladeshi – and Pakistani nationalisms, trauma studies, the European Enlightenment with its attendant rhetoric of progress and development, and the war on terror. The present article locates the novel in the discourse of Bengali nationalism while casting an oblique look at its subversive engagement with some of the representational parameters of Pakistani national discourse. Nationalist discourse constructs binaries, the dominant one being "us" versus "them". In nationalist rhetoric, "us" represents the height of excellence and virtue, while "them" stands for all that is detestable and undesirable, a moral hierarchy in which "us" is always a morally superior entity than its counterpart "them". Mainstream nationalist narratives from post-1971 Bangladesh follow the same representational logic: Pakistanis are mainly represented as murderers and rapists. Bangladeshi cinema concerning the Bangladesh Liberation War of 1971 is a rich archive of such representations, which include Chashi Nazrul Islam's (1972) seminal film *Ora Egaro Jon*. Going against this trend, Rahman's *In the Light of What We Know* represents Pakistanis as human beings torn and traumatized by international forces over which they have little or no control, a depiction that goes against the grain in being more humanistic and historically nuanced. Pakistani national discourse is examined in the novel in the same contra-nationalist light. By challenging negative stereotypes, complex and nuanced depictions such as these can go a long way towards healing past wounds and building a bridge of understanding between seemingly irreconcilable adversaries like Bangladesh and Pakistan or India and Pakistan. Since Rahman's interventionist approach to official national narratives makes his first novel so conspicuous, it is crucial to examine the factors that empower him to construct this intervention. The latter part of the article, therefore, considers Rahman's diasporic location to assess the extent to which it is a shaping factor in his work.

The discursive construction of the nation and its representational coordinates

As Eric Hobsbawm (1992) points out, the birth of a nation depends on a wide range of factors, including "politics, technology and social transformation" (10). From a cultural studies perspective, however, it is commonly recognized that an intimate relationship exists between a nation's coming into existence and the cultural products it generates at the time of its emergence. Conversely, the cultural products that circulate at the time of a nation's birth can themselves significantly contribute to the conception of the nation in question. In recent times the cultural construction of nation has received increased scholarly attention in the historiography of nationalism, a direction pioneered by Benedict Anderson (2006) in his path-breaking study *Imagined Communities: Reflections on the Origin and Spread of Nationalism* (first published in 1983) and Partha Chatterjee's (1993) celebrated postcolonial critique *Nation and Its Fragments: Colonial and Postcolonial Histories.*

Nation formation is always already preceded and accompanied by a particular kind of cultural phenomenon or, to use Michel Foucault's (1972) eloquent term, "discursive formation" (31), which one can characterize as nation-centred or national or nationalist. The same discursive practice continues to flourish in the first few decades of nation building, when the newborn nation operates under a heavy dose of complacency and euphoria. Only after the moment of the nation's arrival has been long left behind (a process which usually takes more than a generation) are the members of a national community able to consider the achievements of their founding fathers with any degree of detachment. This trend usually manifests much earlier and much more readily in diasporic contexts.[1]

Alongside its structural binaries (of which the pitting of "us" against "them" is the most striking), national discourse, irrespective of the geopolitical and temporal setting of its production, is also shaped by several other representational coordinates. Marita Eastmond (1998) identifies one such coordinate and its representational politics in her study of Bosnian Muslim refugees in Sweden: "[t]he construction of significant difference is part of demarcating and legitimating boundaries between groups, and central in all ethnic-nationalist thought" (161). National discourse, in its articulation of nationalist thought, is thus best seen as a battlefield where (typically) two parties are engaged in a conflict to establish the legitimacy of their respective claims over whatever is at stake. The conflicted discursive terrain of nationalism accounts for another of its characteristic features: national discourse in all its manifestations is brazenly biased. In all respects, from morality to cultural practice (such as eating habits), the national "self" encapsulated in "us" is inevitably and unquestionably constructed as far superior to the anti-national "other".

Suppose one takes the example of national discourse that appeared in what used to be East Pakistan (now Bangladesh). In that case, one can readily see how it is structured: innocent Bengalis (the overwhelming majority in East Pakistan) are represented as suffering under a harsh regime run by the West Pakistanis (mainly Punjabis). This representation is hardly a distortion or exaggeration of the reality prevailing in the 1950s and 1960s. However, as bitterness grew between the two wings, both parties began manufacturing stereotypes of each other, highlighting differences that separated them rather than the commonalities that bound them together.[2]

The turn to bitterness began immediately after the emergence of Pakistan. The issue that set the trend in motion concerns the status of the Bengali language in the newly created Pakistani state.[3] The Pakistani ruling elite was mostly non-Bengalis, especially Punjabis. Muhammad Ali Jinnah himself (the father of the Pakistani nation) spoke Gujarati and several other languages but no Bengali at all. His blunt 1948 declaration that "Urdu, and only Urdu" (cited in Umar 1979, 109) would be the state language of Pakistan came as a blow to the Bengalis, who constituted 56 percent of the population at the time. They vehemently protested against this West Pakistani move, seeing it as a threat to their distinct cultural identity. On February 21, 1952, a procession comprising students and civilians demanding equal status for the Bengali language was fired upon by the police, causing several deaths. Two years later, the dismissal of the newly elected government formed by the United Front by Governor-General Ghulam Muhammad so aggravated one of the Front leaders Moulana Bhasani that in his 1957 speech "Salam, Pakistan" (Farewell, Pakistan) (cited in Bahar 2003, 171) he openly called for separation and independence. The 1960s were no better for the relationship between the two wings of Pakistan. Economic disparity, lack of job opportunities for the Bengalis, persecution of the opposition, media censorship, etcetera, led the leaders of Bengali nationalism to conclude that without provincial autonomy the rights of the Bengalis could not be safeguarded. A direct consequence of this realization was the Six-Point Movement organized and launched in 1966 by the Awami League under the leadership of Sheikh Mujibur Rahman. To curb the growing popularity of the Awami League and its charismatic leader, Sheikh Mujibur Rahman was accused in 1968 of separatist politics supposed to be amply aided by India. The case came to be known as the infamous Agartala Conspiracy Case. The strategy backfired and the case was dropped in the face of popular demonstrations. Then came the 1970 general election in which the Awami League captured 160 seats out of 162. Instead of handing over power to Sheikh Mujibur Rahman and his party, General Yahya Khan kept delaying the transfer of power in the name of reconciliation among the contending parties, secretly preparing for a military crackdown which began in March 1971 when the Pakistani army started killing unarmed Bengalis from East Pakistan and raping Bengali women (Saikia 2011). In the wake of these brutalities engulfing the whole of the independent Bengali nation state – as would emerge in less than a year – Quamrul Hassan, a leading Bengali artist, created a poster titled "Annihilate These Demons", which, in the words of Sultana Doula (2016), contains "a monstrous rendition of *Yahya Khan* [sic], the Pakistani president who [in 1971] ordered genocide in Bangladesh" (3; italics in original).

If (West) Pakistanis, especially those in power, came to be identified as demons in the Bengali national imagination in the early 1970s, the tendency does not appear to have changed significantly after many decades. The opening line of Sydney H. Schanberg's (1970) article published in *The New York Times* captures how Bengalis tended to see Pakistanis/Punjabis: "There is an old Bengali saying: If you come across a Punjabi and a snake, kill the Punjabi first" (n.p.). Pakistanis continue to be represented in the same light – that is, as murderers and rapists – in post-1971 Bangladeshi discourse. Even today, as far as I know, there is hardly any difference in imagining the Bangladeshi–Pakistani relationship; however, the situation changed slightly after the Father of the Nation, Bangabandhu Sheikh Mujibur Rahman (b. 1920), was brutally murdered along with most of his family in 1975, with the official narrative covertly becoming more or less pro-Pakistani under the guise of the Islamization process.

How did West Pakistanis view East Pakistanis/Bengalis at the time and how do they now view them (as an independent nation since 1971)? The representation of Bengalis in Pakistani discourse (both now and then) differs only slightly (if at all) from how the former represent their counterparts in most discourses. If, in the Bengali imagination, Pakistanis are demons, the Pakistanis tended to see Bengalis as traitors ever scheming to rupture "the integrity of Pakistan", thus worse than Hindus. In a piece from the early 1970s, James A. Michener (1972) recalls the pejorative terms he had heard Pakistanis employ in talking about Bengalis:

> [I]nvariably, when a West Pakistani spoke of his Bengali fellow national, he did so with the deepest scorn. Indeed, a Punjabi rarely spoke of an Indian Hindu with the contempt he reserved for his fellow Bengali Moslem. "Filthy peasants" was a common description. "Impossible black monkeys" I heard once. If the Bengali had tried to better himself by study he was dismissed as a "book-wallah." If by some miracle he landed a job with the government he was known as an "ink-stained babu" (clerk). (n.p.)

"It was obvious that if this contempt persisted", Michener noted, that a "union between the two halves was going to be imperiled" (n.p.). Michener's premonition proved correct.

Diasporic discourse: The dialectics of nostalgia and critique

In the Light of What We Know originates not from what Homi K. Bhabha (1999) designates as the "nation space" (214) but from the space of a diaspora based in Britain.[4] Rahman's diasporic location requires us to attend to some of the principal characteristics of diasporic discourse – as we did in the case of national discourse earlier.[5] If binaries are one of the structural constituents of national narratives, diasporic ones are marked by ambiguities and inconsistencies, possibly more clearly than most other discourses. One prominent source of these ambivalences and tensions is how diaspora relates to what it calls "home". Those in the diaspora (especially first-generation immigrants) tend to look back at home with nostalgia: everything back home was better and brighter. The parents of Lilia, the protagonist of Jhumpa Lahiri's (1999) short story "When Mr. Pirzada Came to Dine", for example, often complained that in America "[t]he supermarket did not carry mustard oil, doctors did not make house calls, neighbors never dropped by without an invitation" (24). Vijay Mishra (2007) vividly brings out the tension embedded in the diasporic experience:

> They are precariously lodged within an episteme of real or imagined displacements, self-imposed sense of exile; they are haunted by spectres, by ghosts arising from within that encourage irredentist or separatist movements. Diasporas are both celebrated (by late/postmodernity) and maligned (by early modernity). (1)

However, the physical dislocation that is primarily responsible for creating diasporic nostalgia also facilitates a critical look at home. In this respect, as in others, diasporic discourse situates itself as an *other* to national discourse. Diaspora's critical engagement with home manifests itself in its deconstruction of the representational dynamics informing (the imagining of) the nation. Consequently, the representational prejudices and omissions of nationalist thought become visible in the discourse that the diaspora constructs as part of its identity formation. Concerning the two prominent examples from South Asian literary discourse, I shall briefly delineate how diaspora subverts officially sanctioned national narratives before examining Rahman's achievement in his first novel.

My first example comes from *The Shadow Lines*, where Amitav Ghosh (1988) launches a sharp-edged critique of the politics of the Indian national imagination. The novel points to one of the many eloquent silences of Indian national discourse – the 1963–64 communal riots of Kolkata and Dhaka where Ghosh lost an uncle. The daily newspapers of the time did not accord this tragic disturbance as much importance as they did the more celebratory event of the restoration of communal harmony that had been quite fragile in the aftermath of the alleged theft of a lock of the prophet's hair from a shrine in Kashmir. After extensive burrowing in the national archives, the unnamed narrator of *The Shadow Lines* comes across a daily that briefly mentions the Kolkata–Dhaka riots of the early 1960s.

The Pakistani American author Bapsi Sidhwa's (1988) *Ice Candy Man* provides my second example. Sidhwa's work was published in the same year as *The Shadow Lines*, which is not all the two novels have in common. Like Ghosh's novel, *Ice Candy Man* reads the partition of India in 1947 from an angle hardly ever attempted before in the dominant narratives of that most traumatic event in the history of the Indian subcontinent. Mainstream discourse on India's partition represents it as a communal upheaval resulting in an incalculable loss of life and property of the three major communities: Hindus, Muslims, and Sikhs. Other Indian communities, such as Buddhists, Christians, and Parsis, never feature as prominently in the partition stories told (and manufactured) in the nation states of India and Pakistan in their bid to monopolize victimhood. Seen from this perspective, *Ice Candy Man* is a significant intervention in the official representation of India's partition, revising that discourse by revisiting that historic moment from the point of view of a physically challenged eight-year-old Parsi girl named Lenny. Decades after India's falling apart, a diasporic literary text cracks open the Parsi experience of partition.

Those mutually exclusive areas of diasporic and national discourses constitute the spaces where their constructedness and representational politics, more particularly those of national discourse, become exposed. The critical light they shed on each other is one reason why it is so important to compare diasporic and national narratives. The two antagonistic discourses provide a necessary corrective to each other's ideological and representational biases, blemishes, and bluffs.

Reading *In the Light of What We Know* contra-nationally

A contra-nationalist analysis of *In the Light of What We Know* should ideally begin by looking back at Fredric Jameson's (1986) essay "Third-World Literature in the Era of Multinational Capitalism". In this text, Jameson proposes that Third World literary texts (more specifically novels) are basically "national allegories" (69), in which the fortunes of the protagonist symbolize that of the nation to which they belong (and in fact represent). Several postcolonial critics have challenged Jameson's thesis, most notably Aijaz Ahmed (1990). My main purpose in introducing Jameson here is to ask whether, 36 years later, it is appropriate to apply Jameson's formula to texts produced in "Third World" diasporas in so-called developed countries such as Britain or the USA. I am inclined to answer the question with a firm *yes*, for two reasons. First, writers from the diaspora, more often than not, revisit the home they left behind. Home is their recurrent subject (Rushdie 1992). Even second-generation diasporic writers who define home in terms other than those used by their predecessors do not grow out of the nostalgic framework. Second, some diasporic texts themselves strongly encourage a Jamesonian reading – Salman Rushdie's (1981) *Midnight's Children* being a prime example.[6] On both these counts, *In the Light of What We Know* lends itself to the sort of allegorical reading Jameson suggests in his provocative piece. But with a twist! Even though the texts originating from the diasporas located in the Global South are obsessed with the "home" left behind, they frequently try to break loose from the umbilical (national) cord rather than remain attached to it. The situation is comparable to the one so aptly captured in Harold Bloom's (1997) telling phrase "the anxiety of influence", which one may change to "the anxiety of (diasporic) nostalgia", to better suit the diasporic context. And this bittersweet relationship with home provides the diasporic discourse with a rich tension from which the contra-nationalist thrust of Rahman's *In the Light of What We Know* derives its force.

In the Light of What We Know deals with several issues ranging from imperialism to terrorism, and its characters are always on the move across the globe – to London, New York, Kabul, Islamabad, Dhaka, for example. Yet its protagonist Zafar, like its author, is from Bangladesh's north-eastern Sylhet area. Although brought up in Britain, Zafar never belongs there. As for his Bengali identity, he is willing to go to any extent to defend it. The novel records several episodes in which Zafar is seen picking a fight with characters who mistake him for an Indian, despite being told that he was born in Bangladesh. The episode with Tomaso in chapter 16 is perhaps the clearest example.

In October 2014, a couple of months after the publication of *In the Light of What We Know*, Rahman was interviewed by S.S. Haque for *The Oxonian Review*. At one point Haque asked Rahman about the significance of the novel's first two chapters. His answer sheds light on the novel's main concern, as well as the significance of its opening chapters:

> [P]retty much everything in the novel, including its title, is in one way or another in the service of the novel's central line of enquiry: epistemology [...]. It was important, certainly, to bring out early aspects of the novel that run counter to modern trends of mere story-telling. I had to help the reader adopt a stance towards the material as soon as possible that would enable them to get the best experience out of the novel possible.
>
> (Rahman 2014b, n.p.)

The identification of epistemology as the central concern of *In the Light of What We Know* implies that the novel daringly questions all knowledge, discourses, and the way they are constructed, disseminated, and consumed. And quite early on the narrator makes it clear that national discourse is to be put under critical inquiry, thus inviting a reading of the novel in the Jamesonian terms outlined above, though possibly inversely:

> [I]n taking on the task of reporting my conversations with Zafar, of collating and presenting all the material he provided [...] it is the matter of representing details that has most occupied me, the details [...] of his story, which is [...] the story of the breaking of nations, war in the twenty-first century, marriage into the English aristocracy, and the mathematics of love. (Rahman 2014a, 4)

As the story of Zafar and his narrator-friend unfolds, the binary construction of national narratives, the stereotypes they keep generating, the nation and its relationship with its "fragments" (Chatterjee 1993) – particularly women – and so on are taken up for close examination.[7]

As far as Pakistani national discourse is concerned, *In the Light of What We Know* marks a significant intervention.[8] As mentioned above, the primary representational dynamic informing national discourse is the construction of the binary of "us" versus "them". The reason why this binary works so effectively has to do with the process of eliminating differences. Differences in caste, class, community, education, gender, language, and region are subsumed into one overarching identity – national identity. Such national rhetoric systematically keeps out of view the structural inequalities that these differences produce in the society concerned. The whole edifice of national discourse would fall apart if they were spoken of. Hence, one never hears any dissenting voice in the grand narrative of national discourse. One area in which *In the Light of What We Know* parts company with Pakistani national discourse is its depiction of a character who refuses to sing the self-congratulatory national chorus (or anthem).

The father of the narrator of *In the Light of What We Know* was working towards his doctoral degree in America when the Bangladesh Liberation War broke out in 1971.[9] In taking a pro-Pakistani position, the Pakistani diaspora in America revealed the conservative face of diaspora (nationalism) in marked contrast to the subversive positions taken up by the novel's main characters. The narrator's father, for example, stood apart from his compatriots, refusing to join the national herd. Instead, he and his wife "opposed the militarism of the West Pakistani junta and made their feelings known to fellow Pakistanis in Princeton, and farther afield" (Rahman 2014a, 196). The narrator's father even went on to write "a letter to *The New York Times* [...] condemning West Pakistani aggression. To its credit, *The Times* published it" (198). The family had to pay dearly for choosing the untrodden path. The narrator remembers that in Princeton "an aspect of [his] parents' lives was kept at arm's length" (103): "They did not discuss Pakistani politics and they did not discuss Pakistan" (94). They even "received threatening letters" (199). It is only years later that the narrator can figure out the meaning of "the absence of all things Pakistani" in his parents' lives (103): "We had been ostracized" (104). But the father bore it all uncomplainingly:

> The war of 1971 and the holocaust of West Pakistan's conduct in East Pakistan, his criticism of his homeland, the ostracism and then my parents' disengagement – all of this was a history of personal suffering that my father carried with him. (197)

In the Light of What We Know closely examines several stereotypes of Bengalis and Pakistanis frequently present in the mainstream discourses of both nations – the first novel by a member of the Bangladeshi diaspora in England to do so. The novel opens: "In the early hours of one September morning in 2008, there appeared on the doorstep of our home in South Kensington a brown-skinned man" (Rahman 2014a, 3). In the pages that follow, the narrator takes great care to introduce this "brown-skinned man" and explain how the two of them are related. The man, whose name is Zafar, and the narrator (who significantly remains unnamed throughout the novel, perhaps to highlight the importance of the named protagonist in the narrative) were once classmates studying mathematics at Oxford "but that [...] was the beginning and the end of what [they] had in common" (5). The narrator was born into a well-educated, well-to-do family. As already mentioned, his father, a Pakistani, earned his PhD at Princeton before moving to Oxford to "take up a chair in physics" (5). In marked contrast, Zafar is the illegitimate child of a Bengali woman who was raped during the 1971 Bangladesh Liberation War. He was raised in England by one of his maternal uncles and his wife. But: "[t]he greatest difference between us, however [, ...] lay in our social classes" (5). Yet the two classmates ultimately become excellent friends, overcoming the (national) prejudices Bengalis and Pakistanis usually hold against each other back home. Such a friendship is extraordinary because the Bengali–Pakistani relationship, especially after 1971, has routinely been represented as one of mutual antagonism. By depicting it in such a positive light, Rahman not only goes against the orthodox representational dynamics, but also sets up a healthier new trend for himself and his successors.

Rahman does not just substitute friendship for enmity; he goes a step further. It is important to note here that Zafar tells his whole story while staying as a guest in the narrator's South Kensington home. Thus an already beautiful relationship – one built on trust and understanding – is embedded in a broader and more beautiful social relationship – one capable of transcending all "shadow lines", to borrow the title of Ghosh's (1988) novel briefly touched upon above. In most South Asian cultures, the arrival of a guest is considered auspicious, and is often likened to the arrival of Lakshmi, the Hindu goddess of good fortune. The care, humility, and kindness with which a guest is treated in South Asian cultures can be gathered from one well-known literary example. Nikhilesh and Sandip are two friends in Rabindranath Tagore's ([1916] 1919) novel *Ghare Baire* (*The Home and the World*). A *Swadeshi* activist, Sandip comes to stay in his friend's country estate with a view to spreading the gospel of *Swadeshi* and thus procure new recruits for the cause.[10] Over the course of his stay, Sandip falls (or pretends to be) in love with Bimala, his friend's wife, and at one point tries to seduce her. Nikhilesh is repeatedly informed of what is going on in his home under the pretext of *Swadeshi* activism. His guardian-like teacher even asks Nikhilesh to drive away his morally dishonest friend. However, it is only when his friend's duplicity has been unquestionably established that Nikhilesh asks his friend to leave. Such is the standing of a guest in most South Asian cultures.

The stories of the narrator and Zafar in *In the Light of What We Know* intersect at several points. But the one to focus on here concerns the narrator's betrayal of Zafar when he impregnates the latter's fiancée, Emily. What is remarkable about this betrayal is that it does not strain the relationship of the two friends. Nor does it play any significant role in the development of the novel's plot. Towards the end of chapter 19, when Zafar broaches the topic of the narrator's betrayal, he appears neither angry with nor bitter towards him. He simply dismisses the narrator's insistence that he "should say sorry" and offer him "an explanation", because no explanation can alleviate what he, Zafar, has been through (Rahman 2014a, 422–423): this seems to suggest that Zafar has recovered from whatever suffering the narrator's betrayal might have caused him. His decision to stay at his friend's home also points to the same conclusion. One final proof that Zafar holds no grudge against his friend is his willingness to confide his story to him. This willingness is all the more striking because in the moral universe of *In the Light of What We Know* stories are worth fighting for. In a conversation with his son, the narrator's father asks the narrator a rhetorical question: "You know what the most dangerous thing in the world is?" (271). He provides the answer:

> A story, replied my father. I'm not kidding. Stories are dangerous. And I don't mean stories whose messages are capable of endangering. I mean that the form itself is dangerous, not the content. [...] We live in them. We live in this swirling mass of stories written by scribes hidden in some forgotten room up there in the towers. The day someone thought of calling pigeons flying rats was the day the fate of pigeons was sealed. (271)

The conversation gives the reader a measure of the value stories have in the life of the characters. They live by stories they tell about themselves and by the stories others manufacture about them. In such a world, handing over one's stories is more significant than handing over one's material possessions. Thus, in entrusting the narrator with his life story, Zafar is giving away the most precious thing he has ever possessed.

The cultural framing of the narrative in *In the Light of What We Know* regarding friendship and hospitality serves another crucial purpose: it validates the authenticity of the narrator's account of his friend's past life. Because Zafar trusts his friend with his story, readers have no reason to suspect that the story thus transmitted would be tampered with deliberately in its retelling. On several occasions the narrator is seen fussing about the small liberties he has taken in recounting his friend's story. Early in the novel, he insists that "in taking on the task of reporting [his] conversations with Zafar [...] it is the matter of representing details that has occupied [him]" (Rahman 2014a, 4). In assuming the role of a reporter concerned with "representing details", the narrator reassures readers that the narrative that follows will be reliable. These narratorial ruminations are all more or less self-justifications. At the same time, however, they shed light on the narrator's anxiety to deliver faithfully what he has been entrusted with. This metadiscursive consciousness is essentially an expression of humility that not only ensures readers are being offered a trustworthy narrative (the product), but also helps to lay bare its telling (the process). The authors of national discourse rarely, if ever, care to show such humility.

Another subversion of national discourse in *In the Light of What We Know* is its depiction of women characters. In most South Asian national movements, women were involved in huge numbers and the Bangladesh Liberation War was no exception. Bengali women participated in it through many different roles, ranging from cooking for the freedom fighters to fighting alongside them against the Pakistani army. Yet Bengali national discourse portrays women as vulnerable, needing male protection. Even strong women in Bengali national narratives derive their strength from an external source, usually a father or a father figure, a brother or a husband. Their agency is always already derivative and compromised – a representation that clearly shows the shaping influence of patriarchy amply supported by the dominant religious beliefs. Rahman steers clear of this stereotyping of women characters in his novel. None of his women characters is an image of the typical woman deserving admiration of the nation. Nor do they embody the cultural values the nation champions and guards against the encroachment of the regime it is fighting. They are more assertive and independent-minded than their male counterparts, irrespective of the cultural and generational divide.

Apart from the shadowy character whom Zafar meets in his childhood in the place of his birth in Bangladesh, *In the Light of What We Know* has four more or less sharply delineated women characters – two from the generation of the narrator's parents and two from his generation. Because one of the two women characters from the narrator's generation is English and the other from the Pakistani diaspora in Britain, I will take the two women characters from the older generation as my examples. These women, who were born and brought up in a predominantly Islamic cultural environment in South Asia but who are now based in two different (nationally defined) diasporas, present a sharp contrast to the taken-for-granted images of women found in the characteristic narratives of the South Asian nations, including Bangladesh and Pakistan. My first example is the wife of Zafar's maternal uncle who raised him in Britain. The narrator met Zafar's supposed parents only once, on the day Zafar left Oxford after finishing his final exams (Rahman 2014a, 7). It was Zafar's mother whom the narrator found the more interesting (9), as he explains: "Zafar's mother [...] bore herself with a self-assurance I did not see in his father" (7). This self-assurance is also seen in the openness of her comment on Oxford: "[H]ow old everything in Oxford looked. Can't they afford anything new?" (8). These small but crucial details point to the image of a woman far from the stereotype – quiet and soft – found and promoted in national discourse.

The other woman of significance here is the narrator's mother. She possesses all those qualities that the national patriarch would shudder even to imagine in a woman from his cultural background. In marked contrast to his father, whom the narrator thinks of "in a tender way as a bumbling academic, his head in his thoughts", his mother is a "dynamic, pioneering, and assertive woman" (Rahman 2014a, 92), ever ready to embrace elements from other cultures. The narrator is proud that she "bakes that most American of foods, apple pie [...] better than anyone else in the world" (94). Her most outstanding characteristic, however, is her total rejection of Islam – the religion for whose followers Pakistan was created in 1947. The narrator notes:

> My mother [...] had only disdain for religion. Islam, she said, oppressed women and encouraged people to accept their abysmal lot in this world in exchange for the promise of some fanciful happily ever afterlife. Not for her such opiates. (9)

In embracing elements from American (culinary) culture and rejecting Islam altogether, the narrator's mother can be taken to stand for anything but what postcolonial nationalism, at least in its South Asian variety, expects its women, especially mothers, to stand for – the ultimate repository of national culture.

Perhaps the most radical intervention performed by *In the Light of What We Know* is its exposure of the constructedness of Bengali nationalism and the dubious premise that forms the core of Pakistani nationalism. One of the implications of Anderson's (2006) concept of nation as an "imagined community" is that such imagining cannot but be arbitrary – an arbitrariness that has to be kept out of sight by all means. Otherwise, the main objective of the imagining – mobilizing the community members to aspire to independence – could hardly be achieved. While narrating his journey back home to Sylhet, Zafar briefly but insightfully dwells on this issue of Bengali nationalism. His exposition begins with his reflection on the meaning of the country's name: "Bangladesh, or Bangla-desh [...] means Bengali-land" (Rahman 2014a, 67). This innocuous reflection begins to explode like a bomb as one (especially if one happens to be a Bengali) continues reading the whole passage that opens with that reflection. Indeed, Zafar picks up on a detail about Bangladesh whose very mention leaves no doubt about his interventionist stance in regard to the idea of Bengali nationalism. He refers to one particular segment of the Bangladeshi border separating the country from its neighbour, India: "The nation borders the Indian state of West Bengal, whose people also speak Bengali, who *are* also Bengali" (67; original emphasis). The two non-restrictive subordinate clauses following Zafar's remark about the Indian state of West Bengal prompt readers to ask a series of logical questions: if the people of West Bengal are also Bengali and speakers of Bengali, why are they not a nation? Why are they not part of the nation who call themselves Bengali and live in Bangladesh? And why do they belong to a different nation state called India? These questions are a prelude to the question Zafar answers for the reader at the very end of the passage.

Meanwhile, Zafar gives the notion of Bengali national identity one last intriguing twist. This time the allusion is to the poet Tagore who wrote "the national anthems of both India and Bangladesh" (Rahman 2014a, 67). Is Tagore a Bengali or an Indian? Or is he neither but a British (subject)?[11] In the light of what does one decide? So, what distinguishes the Bengali nation from all other nations of the world? What is distinctive about the country called Bangladesh? It is not what the official narratives of the nation trumpet: "Bengali-ness, then, is not a feature that singles out Bangladesh" (67). Tentatively, Zafar suggests that the "Land of Three Rivers might have been more distinctive as a name for the country, a name richer with meaning" (68).[12] If Zafar's questioning of the appropriateness of the country's name serves to highlight its arbitrary nature, it works to serve the same purpose concerning the identity of the country's inhabitants.

Nothing is more challenging and disturbing in this context than the portrayal of Jinnah found in *In the Light of What We Know*. Pakistan was created at the time of the Partition of India in 1947. Jinnah (formerly a committed secularist), and his Muslim League supporters proposed that since Hindus and Muslims belong to two separate religious communities, India should be divided along religious lines. Pakistan – the proposed nation state for the Indian Muslims – is the direct consequence of this political decision. Pakistan was thus imagined as the land of Muslims – a place where they would be free (and were supposed) to observe Islam in all sincerity. But the nationalist rhetoric and on-the-ground reality stand poles apart. Talking about his father's rather eccentric attitude to Islam, the narrator points out:

> Apart from the Friday ritual, my father does not pray, not even once a day, let alone the five times ordained by Sunni Islam. He has never worn a skullcap, my father, and has never shown a drop of guilt for drinking alcohol. (Rahman 2014a, 8)

I have already mentioned how the narrator's mother rejected Islam completely. These two individual cases build up to a revelation about Jinnah few Pakistanis would find admirable and be willing to accept. It is suggested that, in line with the narrator's father, Pakistan's founder had little or no respect for the tenets of Islam. The narrator notes: "[T] he country's founder, Jinnah […] was known to be rather partial to whisky" (9). Though sufficiently cushioned, one can hardly fail to relish the sarcastic tenor of the comment.

Diasporic (dis)location: A shaping factor?

Rahman is a second-generation diaspora writer. This temporal distance from the moment of the Bengali–Pakistani conflict in 1971 enables him to take a critical look at the mainstream national discourses of both parties and thus render visible the representational economy of both. The interventionist perspective facilitated by such temporal distancing derives further strength from Rahman's diasporic location. Physically situated far away from the "nation-space" (Bhabha 1999, 214), he is in a position to shed critical light on the biases and lacunae of nationalist rhetoric that its stakeholders tend to pass over in silence. These spatial and temporal disjunctures help Rahman fashion his engagement with the Bangladeshi and Pakistani official national discourse in the interventionist mode.

Conclusion: Building bridges across national divides

As far as the discourse and ideology of (South Asian) nationalism are concerned, *In the Light of What We Know* represents a breakthrough in Bangladeshi writing in English. Its sophisticated intervention brings to light the constructedness and thus the representational politics of the national narratives of both Bangladesh and Pakistan, especially in terms of the worn-out stereotypes they keep recycling to tarnish the image of each other. Such an intervention can prompt the two nations to engage in what is the most difficult thing: an honest self-reckoning, to pave the way to reconciliation, and then move forward to forging a relationship based not on hatred but on love and mutual understanding. In re-imagining the Bengali–Pakistani relationship, so brilliantly captured in the lasting friendship of Zafar and the narrator, Zia Haider Rahman's first novel has set up a healthy trend which the new generation of writers from both nations will find worth taking further.

Notes

1. Not all scholars see diaspora as progressive (see Carter 2005) and it would be naive to see all diasporas in that light.
2. In Amitav Ghosh's (1988) second novel, *The Shadow Lines*, an ancestral house is so partitioned (due to a family feud between two brothers) that a commode gets bisected in the process.
3. In writing this paragraph, I have extensively borrowed from secondary sources which include Guru Saday Batabyal (2021), Sanjay K. Bhardwaj (2010), and Willem V. Schendel (2009).
4. From Bhabha's perspective, both nation and diaspora are spaces where identity is a performance, not a given.

5. Diaspora has been variously defined by scholars. The concept has evolved from William Safran's (1991) focus on geographically dispersed communities such as the Jews to the broader definitions of James Clifford (1994) ("the term *diaspora* is a signifier" [308]), Arjun Appadurai (1996), Bhabha (1990, 1994), and Stuart Hall (1990).
6. The work of Rohinton Mistry (b. 1952) is another good example.
7. Most postcolonial nationalisms, including Indian nationalism, are haunted by the ghosts of old patriarchy; hence women's marginal or "fragmentary" status in the scheme of things set up by the national elite.
8. Not all diasporic discourse is interventionist (see, for example, Anam 2007).
9. Mr Pirzada was also working on his research project in Lahiri's (1999) short story "When Mr. Pirzada Came to Dine" (23–42).
10. The *Swadeshi* movement was an early-20th-century anti-British movement in India, geared to boycotting European/British goods.
11. Tagore (1861–1941) was born and died during the British rule of India.
12. Zafar is perhaps drawing a parallel here with the Punjab, the land of five rivers.

Acknowledgements

An embryonic version of this article was presented at the "Multilingualism and the Bangladeshi Culture" session at the Modern Language Association (MLA) Convention 2022 held online on January 6, 2022.

Disclosure statement

No potential conflict of interest was reported by the author.

References

Ahmed, Aijaz. 1990. "Jameson's Rhetoric of Otherness and the 'National Allegory'." In *In Theory: Classes, Nations, Literatures*, and Aijaz Ahmed, 95–122. London and New York: Verso.

Anam, Tahmima. 2007. *A Golden Age*. London: John Murray.

Anderson, Benedict. 2006. *Imagined Communities: Reflections on the Origin and Spread of Nationalism*. 2nd ed. London and New York: Verso.

Appadurai, Arjun. 1996. *Modernity at Large: Cultural Dimensions of Globalization*. Minneapolis, MN: University of Minnesota Press.

Bahar, Abid S. 2003. "The Religious and Philosophical Basis of Bhasani's Political Leadership." PhD diss., Concordia U. https://spectrum.library.concordia.ca/id/eprint/2294/1/NQ85265.pdf

Batabyal, Guru Saday. 2021. "Politics in Pakistan and the Bangladesh Liberation War, 1971." *Journal of Defence Studies* 15 (4): 35–57.

Bhabha, Homi K., ed. 1990. *Nation and Narration*. London: Routledge.

Bhabha, Homi K. 1994. *The Location of Culture*. London and New York: Routledge.

Bhabha, Homi K. 1999. "DissemiNation: Time, Narrative and the Margins of the Modern Nation." In *The Blackwell Reader in Contemporary Social Theory*, edited by Anthony Elliot, 211–219. Malden, MA and Oxford: Blackwell.

Bhardwaj, Sanjay K. 2010. "Contesting Identities in Bangladesh: A Study of Secular and Religious Frontiers." Working Paper 36. Asia Research Centre. London School of Economics and Political Science. https://eprints.lse.ac.uk/38640/1/ARCWP36-Bhardwaj.pdf

Bloom, Harold. 1997. *The Anxiety of Influence: A Theory of Poetry*. 2nd ed. New York and Oxford: Oxford University Press.

Carter, Sean. 2005. "The Geopolitics of Diaspora." *Area* 37 (1): 54–63. doi:10.1111/j.1475-4762.2005.00601.x.

Chatterjee, Partha. 1993. *Nation and Its Fragments: Colonial and Postcolonial Histories*. Princeton, NJ: Princeton University Press.

Clifford, James. 1994. "Diasporas." *Cultural Anthropology* 9 (3): 302–338. doi:10.1525/can.1994.9.3.02a00040.

Doula, Sultana. 2016. "Quamrul Hassan, His Colors, Paintings & Women." Final Informative Paper, University of Development Alternative, Dhaka, Bangladesh, March 29. https://www.academia.edu/33007848/Quamrul_Hassan_his_Colors_Paintings_and_Women_by_Sultana_Doula

Eastmond, Marita. 1998. "Nationalist Discourses and the Construction of Difference: Bosnian Muslims Refugees in Sweden." *Journal of Refugee Studies* 11 (2): 161–181. doi:10.1093/jrs/11.2.161.

Foucault, Michel. 1972. *The Archaeology of Knowledge and the Discourse on Language*, Translated by A.M. Sheridan Smith. New York: Pantheon Books.

Ghosh, Amitav. 1988. *The Shadow Lines*. Boston, MA: Houghton Mifflin.

Hall, Stuart. 1990. "Cultural Identity and Diaspora." In *Identity: Community, Culture, Difference*, edited by Jonathan Rutherford, 222–237. London: Lawrence and Wishart.

Hobsbawm, Eric J. 1992. *Nations and Nationalism since 1780: Programme, Myth, Reality*. 2nd ed. Cambridge: Cambridge University Press.

Islam, Chashi Nazrul, dir. 1972. *Ora Egaro Jon*. Dhaka: Star Film Corporation Ltd.

Jameson, Fredric. 1986. "Third-World Literature in the Era of Multinational Capitalism." *Social Text* 15 (Autumn): 65–88. doi:10.2307/466493.

Lahiri, Jhumpa. 1999. "When Mr. Pirzada Came to Dine." In *Interpreter of Maladies*, and Jhumpa Lahiri, 23–42. Boston, MA and New York: Houghton Mifflin Harcourt.

Michener, James A. 1972. "A Lament for Pakistan." *The New York Times*, January 1. https://www.nytimes.com/1972/01/09/archives/a-lament-for-pakistan-the-two-pakistans-had-only-religion-in-common.html

Mishra, Vijay. 2007. *The Literature of the Indian Diaspora: Theorizing the Diasporic Imaginary*. London and New York: Routledge.

Rahman, Zia Haider. 2014a. *In the Light of What We Know*. New York: Farrar, Straus and Giroux.

Rahman, Zia Haider. 2014b. "The Completeness of Novel-Writing and Inquiries into Epistemology: Zia Haider Rahman Talks to S.S. Haque." *The Oxonian Review* 26 (2). https://www.oxonianreview.org/wp/zia-haider-rahman-interview/.

Rushdie, Salman. 1981. *Midnight's Children*. London: Jonathan Cape.

Rushdie, Salman. 1992. *Imaginary Homelands: Essays and Criticisms 1981–1991*. London: Granta Books.

Safran, William. 1991. "Diasporas in Modern Societies: Myths of Homeland and Return." *Diaspora: A Journal of Transnational Studies* 1 (1): 83–99. doi:10.1353/dsp.1991.0004.

Saikia, Yasmin. 2011. *Women, War, and the Making of Bangladesh: Remembering 1971*. Durham, NC: Duke University Press.

Schanberg, Sydney H. 1970. "The Bengalis and the Punjabis: Nation Split by Geography, Hate." *The New York Times*, December 4. https://www.nytimes.com/1970/12/04/archives/the-bengalis-and-the-punjabis-nation-split-by-geography-hate.html

Schendel, Willem V. 2009. *A History of Bangladesh*. Cambridge: Cambridge University Press.

Sidhwa, Bapsi. 1988. *Ice Candy Man.* New Delhi: Penguin.
Tagore, Rabindranath. 19161919. *The Home and the World,* Translated by Surendranath Tagore. London: Macmillan.
Umar, Badruddin. 1979. *Purbo-Banglar Bhasha Andolon O Totkalin Rajniti* [The Language Movement of East Bengal and Contemporary Politics]. Dhaka: Agamee Prakashani.

Introducing a Bangladeshi Writer in English: An Interview with Kaiser Haq

Mohammad A. Quayum

Kaiser Haq was born in 1950 in Dhaka, Bangladesh. He was educated at Dhaka University, where he took his BA (Honours) and MA in English, and Warwick University, where he took a Ph.D. as a Commonwealth Scholar. His thesis was a critical biography of the Australian-born writer Frederic Manning. He fought in the War of Independence in 1971 as a Lieutenant in the Bangladesh Liberation Army. He has been on the English faculty of Dhaka University since 1975, and is currently a Professor. He was a Senior Fulbright Scholar at the Centre for Twentieth Century Studies, University of Wisconsin-Milwaukee in 1986-87. During 1996-97 he was Regional Chairperson (Eurasia) for the Commonwealth Writers Prize.

He has published four collections of poetry: *Starting Lines* (Liberty, Dhaka, 1978), *A Little Ado* (Granthabithi, Dhaka, 1978), *A Happy Farewell* (University Press Ltd., Dhaka, 1994), *Black Orchid* (Aark Arts, London, 1996); translated *Selected Poems of Shamsur Rahman* (BRAC, Dhaka, 1985) and Tagore's *Quartet (Chaturanga,* Heinemann, Asian Writers Series, 1993); and edited an anthology, *Contemporary Indian Poetry* (Ohio State University Press, 1990). His latest book, forthcoming in 1997 from Peepal Tree Books, Leeds, is *The Wonders of Vilayet,* an English version of an eight-eenth-century Indian traveller's memoir of Europe.

Haq is a regular contributor to *London Magazine,* and has also appeared in a number of periodicals, among them: UK: *Chapman, Wasafiri, Acumen, The Journal of Commonwealth Literature, Midland Poetry Worksheet, Interarts, Literature Matters, The Cambridge Review, Poetry from Warwick, South Asia Research, The Main Street Journal;* Singapore: *WLWE;* India: *New Quest, Literature Alive.*

He has been anthologized in *The Arnold Anthology of Post-Colonial Literatures in English* (1996), *Stories from South Asia* (OUP, 1988J, *The Worlds of Muslim Imagination* (Islamabad, 1986), *Imagine* (Oslo, 1990), *Contemporary Literary Criticism* (USA).

His current projects include an autobiography, an edition of Frederic Manning's poetry and prose, and a translation of Tagore's novel, *Yogayog.*

****

Tell us something about the state of English and English writing in Bangladesh. Why has Bangladesh not produced a sizable body of English writing since independence?

Bangladesh doesn't have much of an anglophone tradition. If you take the trouble of looking up the entries on Bangladesh in the Routledge Encyclopaedia of Post-Colonial Literatures in English you will know what I mean. It was reported to me that when Ian Hamilton was putting together the *Oxford Companion to Twentieth Century Poetry in English,* he was dismayed at not being able to get in a decent number of entries on

Bangladeshi writers. All the readable poetry, fiction and non-fictional prose in English by Bangladeshi writers could be accommodated in a single volume. As for the vast majority of Bangladeshi English writings, their perpetrators do not handle their chosen medium as one would a first language; nor as a second language; nor even as a foreign language. The language is, simply, utterly foreign to them. On the map of South Asian anglophone literature Bangladesh is very much on the fringe, more so than Pakistan or Sri Lanka. Our tiny English-language publishing industry survives on editions of dissertations on the social sciences subsidized by aid agencies. Of the handful of literary works in English, most have been privately printed, and none has covered the costs.

Though Bangladesh used to be part of British Bengal, the most Westernized and cosmopolitan part of the Raj, it has since been transformed by lingual nationalism into a virtually monoglot state proud of the thousand year-old literary tradition that it shares with West Bengal and Tripura. Its self-appointed cultural commissars ritually inveigh against *apasanskriti* (perverse culture) by which they mean Western culture.

Are you optimistic about the future of English writing in Bangladesh?

No - my answer follows from what I have already said. Individual Bangladeshis still trying to write in English work in isolation. Nor can one envisage an anglophone literary community evolving here.

You started writing in the early 70s, immediately after the country's liberation war, when the trend was for writers as well as for academics, to vociferously defend the mother tongue and, under the spell of an ultra-nationalist sentiment, reject English as well as Urdu as the language of the oppressors. Why did you decide to write in English in an atmosphere like that?

Actually, I started writing in 1966 or 1967, when I was finishing secondary school. I do not think I would have tried creative writing in English if I weren't an English-medium boy. Pondering this aspect of my identity led me to look up the hyphenated compound in the new edition of the OED. It wasn't there. "English-medium," which to us epitomizes the lingering cultural legacy of the Raj is not really English! It is Indian English and, I believe, not a very old coinage either. In British India a large proportion of secondary schools, known as "High English" (H.E. for short) schools imparted education through the medium of English. For years all of them used certain standard texts, like Nesfield's *Grammar,* Hall and Stevens's *Geometry,* Jadav's *Arithmetic,* etc. These schools were scattered all over the subcontinent, making it possible for many students in remote villages to attend them. With independence these schools adopted subcontinental vernaculars as the medium of instruction. But English was retained by a small number of schools, concentrated in the cities. The compound "English-medium" was - correct me if I am wrong - coined to refer to these schools. Because of the altered social conditions these have acquired a significance the old "High English" schools did not have.

English-medium schools are elitist and relatively pricey and have fostered a distinctive cosmopolitan ethos whose exemplars use English as if it were their first language, a "foster mother-tongue," as an Indian poet has put it, and are somewhat supercilious towards the vernacular-educated. "English- mediumness" has been given pointed fictional expression through Upamanyu Chatterjee's grouchy protagonist in *English, August,* and generally pervades contemporary subcontinental writing in English; the rhyming Chatterjees in *A Suitable Boy* are a more personable English-medium brood. There is an influential English-medium class, spread thinly over the subcontinent and beyond, wherever there are South Asian settlers. One of them, Salman Rushdie, has used the term with all its connotative resonance in his latest novel. It cannot be long before a supplement to the new OED picks it up.

An English-medium boy or girl who catches the creative-writing bug becomes an Indo-Anglian. This too is a recent Indian English coinage, and not a felicitous one either, though one could argue in its favour that its awkwardness reflects the nature of what it designates. Besides, it has got into the new OED, which notes that it refers to (i) literature in English produced by Indians, and (ii) an Indian producing such literature. A broader usage is noticeable at times, e.g. when M. J. Akbar in a book review describes Mr. Jinnah as a person of "impeccable Indo-Anglian tastes": witness his natty suits and chhota whiskey at sundown, not to mention his pukka accent. In this sense "English-medium" and "Indo-Anglian" become interchangeable. From a literary critical angle, though, it is advisable to restrict the latter to subcontinental (and not just Indian) writers and writing.

But how did I get to writing in English - and poetry at that? I wasn't a great poetry buff in school. The great English poets - Milton, Wordsworth, Byron, Shelley, Keats - were names to remember and drop at opportune moments. But what we read by them didn't particularly appeal - a common experience in the tropics, it seems. Naipaul points out how English literature as encountered by "us" is "like an alien mythology. There was, for instance, Wordsworth's notorious poem about the daffodil. A pretty flower, no doubt; but we had never seen it. Could the poem have any meaning for us?" Once a friend got me interested in Shelley by whispering that he had written a poem in which occurred the phrase "The golden tresses between her thighs." A futile search in the school library followed. I still haven't discovered the source of this exciting line. If anyone can help I. shall be most grateful.

Besides the flora and fauna there is the prosody of traditional English verse. It is alien to us. Just note how awkwardly our students read it. Their difficulty is exacerbated by the fact that subcontinental English, though an identifiable linguistic phenomenon, has not yet evolved a standard form - in the sense there is a "standard" form of British or American English. Just listen to an English language-learners' tape produced in India and you will know what *I* mean.

Then I had something like a conversion experience. Our literature classes at St Gregory's were taken by Brother Hobart, a lovable Irish-American eccentric, one of the most remarkable personalities I have known. He would take a poem and draw the whole class into the exercise of producing a critical appreciation. What sort of poem is it? Who is saying what and to whom? What do the similes and metaphors say to us? Asking such questions, trying out answers, modifying them, he would write out a response to the poem on the blackboard. He taught me that writing was a process of playing around with words till one struck what seemed the right note. Moving from poem to poem in our textbook we came to Lawrence's "Snake." And it opened up a whole new world. I could feel the music of its free verse as I hadn't felt the music of any other English poem. Its simple diction gave me immediate access to the drama enacted by human education and primordial sympathies. That I had never seen a carob-tree hardly mattered; the adjectival fanfare preceding it - "the deep, strange-scented shade of the great dark carob-tree" - brought it to life. I started scribbling free verse. Walking in the park I began a poem, "Nature on a leash." Friends applauded. I began enjoying myself in my new role. I do not wish to make too much of this experience, but it may not be far-fetched to hypothesize that similar experiences must be quite common in the Third World; the fact that most Third World English poetry is in free verse would seem to support the hypothesis.

You yourself actively took part in the country's liberation war. Is there any incident or incidents you wish to recollect for us from that experience? Did the war in any way contribute to your poetic life?

I was an undergraduate when the war broke out, and like thousands of my generation I made the existential choice of taking up arms to fight for an independent Bangladesh. Perhaps the most memorable combat incident was when a friend, a fellow company commander - our companies were in defensive positions facing Pakistani fortifications in two neighbouring villages - wanted to see me one morning and decided to take a short cut across a field - and got hit by a sniper. One of my boys rushed to me and in a panic-stricken voice gave me the news. I went at once and saw my friend lying in the middle of the field. Fortunately, as I later saw, the bullet had gone clean through his arm, without touching the bone, and he had only been stunned. But the sniper was still firing away and he didn't have the strength to move unaided. I ran to him and somehow dragged him to the cover provided by the trunk of a dismembered tree. The sniper's bullet now rhythmically hit the timber, making a ringing noise. I shouted for an LMG - a light machine gun - and one of my boys raced to us with one. I figured out that the sniper was perched on a tree and fired a burst at it. At once his bullets stopped making music against the tree trunk. With the cover I could provide with the LMG, my friend was now carried to safety - and to hospital.

There were many exciting moments, and memorable characters. But curiously, I have written only couple of poems about the war.

It is a bit surprising that you have not written more poems about your war-time experience. Do you find the experience too violent and destructive for creative purposes? Does it create a chilling effect on your imagination and do you feel, as for example, Kurt Vonnegut did about the massacre of Dresden during the second World War, which he had witnessed first hand, that "there is nothing intelligent to say about a massacre?"

I think there are two reasons. The first is literary. There is such an impressive body of war poems in English, especially from the First World War, that it probably had an inhibiting effect on my creativity. This is mere speculation, I admit. The other reason has to do with what one might call the cultural concomitant of the war. The war had generated so much of a rhetorical smoke-screen, that it has become nearly impossible to bring it into sharp focus. But I haven't given up the hope of doing so.

Your poems range from personal ruminations about life and death to interpersonal and social criticisms. Since your interests are so diverse, may I ask you what is of foremost importance to you as a poet? Do you write with any ulterior objective like improving self or society as, for example, did some of the nineteenth century poets? I am of course thinking of poets like Shelley, Whitman or even Matthew Arnold, who in his vision ofa "high destiny" for poetry, endowed the poet with the responsibility of "teacher" or "preacher".

It's a big question, but my answer will be short. I don't have any of those grand, "ulterior" objectives. The nineteenth century is long gone, and as we prepare to step into the twenty-first, the most I can hope for is to clarify certain aspects of my experience - for myself and the handful of people who care to read me.

Who are your most favourite poets? Do you draw your inspiration from any of the Bengali poets or from Bengali poetry as such?

Eliot, Lawrence, Auden, Larkin, Enright, Baudelaire, Rilke, Neruda, Octavia Paz, William Carlos Williams, Wallace Stevens, Frank O'Hara, Walcott, Nissim Ezekiel, Dom Moraes. None, as you can see, is Bengali.

What about Tagore and Shamsur Rahman? 1 notice that you have left out both the writers from your list although you have translated both. In case of Tagore perhaps your appreciation for his prose is greater than for his poetry. Am I right?

I respect both poets, but neither is a direct inspiration. Nor is modem Bengali poetry in general, even though I have read quite a bit of it with pleasure. Tagore's poetry is romantic, and seems a bit remote to the contemporary reader. You're right in thinking I like his prose better -I can relate to it more readily, and, I believe, so can the contemporary reader-at-large.

I must say that I specially like your humorous poems and poems in which you experiment with Subcontinental English. Is humour important for a poet and how do you decide, when you write a poem, whether you will write it in a serious or humorous vein? Is it a matter of choice or spontaneity?

The humour comes spontaneously. I am fond of the comic.

What is your feeling about Subcontinental English? Do you think it will by and by gain recognition as has, for example, some of the other varieties of English?

There are many kinds of Subcontinental English. They range from pidgin to Modified Standard. Following Ezekiel's lead I have written a few comic poems in demotic Subcontinental English. Subcontinental literature in English will naturally exploit the various kinds of English spoken in the region alongside Standard English. By now it has become quite respectable to do so.

Do you write with any specific readership in mind or just for your therapeutic need and pleasure? What do you think is the significance of a poet in English in a country like Bangladesh that is largely mono-lingual and mono-cultural?

By now every third world writer in English is aware of a worldwide readership, whether potential or real - and so do I. This readership includes people in Bangladesh, since serious readers in the country are bilingual; they read in Bengali as well as English. I hope at least a few readers in Bangladesh will find my work interesting.

Some of your poems do really bring into focus the present state of reality in the country, with its hypocrisy, corruption, oppression and as you call it the "debris of downtroddendom." Do you see any respite from all these in the foreseeable future?

No.

Would you like to elaborate on your view, please.

I'd rather not. But if you insist I'll say that the political and economic scene in Bangladesh does not provide any grounds for optimism.

Of course, you are not only a poet but also a translator and editor. You have translated several Bengali works into English, including Tagore's Quartet *and the poetry of Shamsur Rahman. Do you enjoy translating and find translation a creative exercise or is it something that we need to do for bridging cultures?*

Translating from Bengali has a special significance for me. Since my literary sensibility has two rather distinct areas, one occupied by Bengali literature, the other by literature in English, translating is a way of unifying the two. It is also a means of coming to terms with aspects of myself of which I may have been only vaguely aware, and of combining the creative and critical sides of my mind: Pound, you may recall, cites translation as a mode of criticism.

My translation have all been labours of love: Shamsur Rahman and Shaheed Quaderi, dear friends besides being leading Bengali poets; *The Wonders of Vilayet,* an eighteenth century Indian's memoir of a trip to Britain which is appearing this year (1997) from Peepal Tree Books in Leeds; Tagore's *Chaturanga (Quartet).* And in a sabbatical year that has just begun I plan to translate Tagore's *Yogayog.*

Generally speaking, I find translating Bengali prose a more satisfying activity than translating the poetry, partly because more is lost in translating poetry, partly because I don't think Bengali poetry adds much that is original to the body of world literature. The prose, on the other hand, incorporates more of the complex texture of our culture and is therefore likely to appeal to readers interested in otherness. Doesn't Richard Rorty in *Irony, Contingency, Solidarity* make a case for novels and documentaries as the best agents available for broadening and deepening our human sympathies?

Tell us something about the works you have translated.

Translating Tagore's *Quartet* led me to realize with blinding clarity the extent to which the Bengali psyche - and indeed my individual psyche - is polarised between the devotional and romantic on the one hand, and the logical and rational on the other. We have all been aware of the impact of *bhakti* (devotional mysticism) with its associated irrationalism and eroticism on the Bengali mind. We are perhaps less aware of our logic-chopping side, which goes back at least as far as the Navya-Nyaya logicians of the sixteenth century. It is conspicuous today as what Alan Ross in a poem titled "Bengal" calls "A querulous literacy." The opposition between the two *weltanschuungs* passed into popular culture, as in the saying, *"Biswasay milai swarga, twarkay bahudur"* ("Faith takes you to heaven, but arguments lead you astray"). I recall it from my childhood. In its original form it has "Krishna" instead of "swarga" ("heaven") and obviously a *bhakti* squib directed at the hair-splitting logicians. By substituting "swarga" for "Krishna," Muslims too could use the proverb: an interesting example of how the two religious communities could drink from the fount of a shared culture.

Sadly, the two aspects of the Bengali psyche seem to have remained separate throughout history: ours has always been a dissociated sensibility. I like to think that in writing in and translating into English - an activity that as Meenakshi Mukherjee pointed out years ago, enhances our critical awareness of the complexities of our cultural inheritance - I also try to bring the disparate parts into a meaningful dialogic relationship.

The Wonders of Vilayet, which is due to come out, is a translation of the first account of the West by an Indian who went there in 1766-69. The Indian was a *munshi,* a scribe, a pre-modem Oriental, and it is fascinating to see how he describes and interprets his experiences. I could recognize in him an ancestor. Also, he is very like the uneducated or little educated subcontinental of today in his attitudes. I could identify a little with him; at the same time he seemed quite alien. Amidst the Said-inspired hullabaloo over Orientalism I could see him as part of a feeble countercurrent that has not yet been adequately studied.

I notice that after two decades of engagement in poetry, you have now decided to diversify into prose. You are currently writing your autobiography. How far are you with this project and what will be its main focus? Will it be your "inner" life or your "outer" life?

It will deal with both my "inner" life and my "outer" life; I have finished a long essay on my father's experiences in the Second World War listening to my father talk about the war in my childhood was a fascinating experience, and this essay is a sort of prelude to my own story. The rest is still in an embryonic state. I may end up with a collection of essays rather than a more unified book. Incidentally, it isn't just now that I've become interested in writing prose. Prose has always interested me - especially the essay form, which I feel is sadly neglected nowadays.

Thank you very much, Kaiser Haq.

Delving beneath the surface: An interview with Monica Ali

Sadaf Saaz

ABSTRACT

Monica Ali is widely recognized as a trailblazer for writers of Bangladeshi origin in English. She published her bestselling debut novel *Brick Lane* in 2003 and went on to write three more works of fiction: *Alentejo Blue* (2006), *In the Kitchen* (2009), and *Untold Story* (2011). In this interview conducted in autumn 2021, she discusses her recent novel, *Love Marriage*, which depicts two families from different backgrounds in contemporary Britain: Bengali Indian Muslim and white Christian British. Other topics include Monica Ali's writing process, why she writes, the experience of her dual heritage, her thoughts on feminism, and her exploration of class and race in today's multicultural Britain. This was Ali's first interview after writing *Love Marriage*, which hit the book stands a few months later in February 2022. The novel has been well reviewed and critically acclaimed and looks set to have the popular appeal of her classic novel, *Brick Lane*.

Introduction: Monica Ali's writing career

Monica Ali is best known for *Brick Lane* (Ali 2003), her novel about the Bangladeshi community in the UK and Bangladesh; it has a young Bangladeshi woman, Nazneen, as the protagonist. Monica Ali was named one of the 20 best young British novelists by *Granta Magazine* in 2003, and *Brick Lane* was shortlisted for the Booker Prize and nominated for the National Book Critics Circle and *Los Angeles Times* Book Award. It has been translated into 26 languages and been made into a film. In 2019 Ali was elected a Fellow of the Royal Society of Literature.

After the global success of her first book, Monica Ali did not follow the trajectory that many were perhaps expecting, of continuing to write about the Bangladeshi community. Her second novel, *Alentejo Blue* (Ali 2006), set in a Portuguese village, further explores displacement, tracing the impact of modernization from the perspective of those within the village and from "elsewhere", through her keenly observed and finely constructed characters. In *In the Kitchen* (Ali 2009), her third novel, Ali interrogates class, the immigrant experience, and their intersections, all told through a compelling plot revolving around the characters in a hotel restaurant. *Untold Story* (Ali 2011) was inspired by the life of Princess Diana (1961–97); it looks at the assumptions by which women are generally judged and raises questions about identity and the phenomenon of celebrity. Ali's latest work, *Love Marriage: A Novel* (Ali 2022), appears more than a decade after

Untold Story. She has continually refused to be boxed in by postcolonial expectations of what she should be writing about and explores the essence of human relationships and the way they play out in the different circumstances life throws up, in diverse settings, topics, and contexts.

I recently rediscovered a copy of *Brick Lane*, purchased on a trip to London in July 2003, which I had forgotten to get Ali to sign during her trip to Dhaka on the occasion of the ninth Dhaka Lit Fest (November 7–9, 2019). We had a delightful conversation on the stage of the Bangla Academy, and it was wonderful to see Dhaka audiences meet Ali, one of the first Bangladeshi-born authors writing in English to have received international acclaim. This interview is based on three separate but interlinked telephone conversations spanning more than four hours, in autumn 2021. At that point, *Love Marriage* had just been printed and I am grateful to Monica Ali for couriering me a copy for this interview.

Sadaf Saaz (SS): I have just finished reading your new novel *Love Marriage*, which I couldn't put down. In a world seemingly full of extremes, you normalized things and showed a multicultural society that is organic.

Monica Ali (MA): I think there might be a line somewhere in the book that talks about the world not being black and white; it's not, is it? Increasingly it is a world where we all exist in our own little echo chambers, "coms" bubbles, and we are starting to believe in oversimplifications. I think this happens on both sides of the political divide and even in fiction. Richard Powers (2021), in his novel *Bewilderment*, creates a world in the near future, in which there is a caricature of a Trump-like character to say that everybody on the "other" side of the echo-wars has evil motives. Well, life isn't actually like that. People have very complicated sets of reasons as to why they might be in favour of, say, the coal industry; maybe they are concerned about the employment of their husbands. If one has even the vaguest intention of giving us the feeling of life itself, then the duty of the novelist is to go into those complexities. That's what makes reading fiction interesting for me, when I find it in other novels. That's when I get really engaged. I guess you are always trying to write that book that you would like to read! Yes, I am pleased that that's spoken to you as well.

SS: You are interested in the perspective of each one of these characters?

MA: Yes, I mean, obviously, the characters don't bear equal weight in the book in terms of "time on stage" or access to all of their interiority, but I am interested in each and every one of them. Otherwise, what is the point of writing? They just become like puppets on a stage rather than fully inhabited. The goal is to inhabit those other mindsets. There's been research done about people who read fiction; it's been shown that one can increase powers of empathy through reading novels, and that can't come about unless the writer has had that experience herself to produce the work. I'm not deluded enough to think I can have any real impact in the world; nevertheless, there is a moral dimension for me.

SS: I felt it was a story of the Britain of today.

MA: I am really hoping that some of these things come out, as you say, in an organic way which comes spontaneously out of character, rather than feeling superimposed. To me, it is about who we are and how we love in Britain today. Even though it's particular in its Britishness, I think those things translate well – it remains to be seen – but those themes of duty to one's parents versus following one's heart – whether that's in marital terms or in career terms or other matters – apply all over the world to a greater or lesser extent, and the conflict between generations, issues about sex and how it relates to your own identity. There are so many unities that are afforded through what is sometimes written off as the "domestic sphere".

I am a big Jane Austen fan, and she wrote endlessly about engagements and marriages and courtship rituals, but she was also incredibly sharp about power and where power resides, and about money. She is very specific about who earns how much and where it comes from. She has a lot to say about class; very finely observed gradations between the classes, even *within* the upper echelons. She captures all of that, and the role of women. Today we are in a very different landscape; it's multicultural; women go out to work. In *Love Marriage*, Yasmin is a doctor and all of that. Nevertheless, there is the same opportunity to explore cultural and social issues through what marriage means, the expectations surrounding it, the customs surrounding it, how the families fit together, the differences in class, who's going to pay for what; I mean there is endless opportunity there, and it doesn't have to be force-fitted.

SS: Yes, absolutely, all of these are things that we are confronted with ...

MA: Yes, and they're messy, aren't they?

SS: Oh, totally. The title of the book itself is interesting. "Love marriage" is such a loaded term that I thought it was a very clever title.

MA: I'm generally not good at titles, but I was really pleased with this one, because I think it could be read in different ways, depending on how you punctuate it in your head. I mean, it could be love, marriage, where love has to be the precursor of marriage. Or run together as symbiotically connected? Or run together as a command! It could be love marriage as in not an arranged marriage. I mean, in the UK, a love marriage is just called marriage because it's the norm. And the other kind of marriage is called an arranged marriage. But in Bangladesh, or most of Asia, an arranged marriage is called simply – marriage. Because it's the norm. And what we here in the UK call marriage is labelled as love marriage there. So the words signal different meanings, and I quite enjoy that. A lot of British readers won't get that, but that's okay.

SS: Your protagonist Yasmin has a Bengali Muslim heritage, and the story is set in multicultural London. Is this book coming full circle or something like that, bringing aspects of the duality of your heritage, which you have said has had a big influence on you?

MA: I mean, everything has some sort of influence, so it's kind of an artificial exercise to me. About circling back, I have been wondering if people will say, she's had to go back to writing about brown people because nobody was interested in her other books. I actually don't see it that way at all, and if so, does it matter what people think about that?

Brick Lane and its environment is very monocultural. I'm imagining that critics and readers will be saying, she's gone back to where she started, and whether Iwill find that irritating in the way Yasmin does at the gala dinner when one of Harriet's friends just assumes that she's Hindu, because we are "all the same". Brown people are not all the same. Yasmin's father is adoctor. He speaks very good English, and she's also adoctor, so they're in adifferent social class. There are some echoes there as there would be in any white writer writing about family dynamics from one book to the next. It's automatically granted that every white British family is unique.

I've drawn those parallels before when I've talked about people being shocked that I wrote a novel inspired by Princess Diana; it's like – what on earth are you doing writing about a white princess? I've drawn out the deep underlying resonances for me, about Lydia (my fictional princess in *Untold Story*) being an uneducated, virgin bride as Nazneen was, married to a much older man, very much under the scrutiny of a wider community, rebelling, having an affair, then finding that a man isn't the way to remake her life, and pursuing her own identity. Nobody has said to me, but you're just writing the same story again. There are certain differences, which are to do with skin colour, because that's mainly what people will see. I can't blame them for that; it's just that they don't think about it.

There is a very significant connection for me between Lydia and Nazneen. The germ of the idea of why I wanted to write about those two protagonists comes from the same place. Nazneen is a brown woman, a Bangladeshi housewife, a woman in a sari, who doesn't speak much English. It's very easy for the casual observer to dismiss somebody like her as not even fully human, and maybe not grant her the complexity of a deep interior life. For Lydia, I was interested in exploring the other extreme, which is about celebrity and its commodification – but ultimately, it's about the propensity of the casual observer to dismiss that person who has everything in the world, who is so different from Nazneen in every way, except that she is also not granted her full humanity. And that's where my interest comes from.

SS: You manage to tackle broader issues through their lives ...

MA: I think we are hardwired for stories. People have been telling stories since the caveman era, drawing around the fire. I like a strong narrative, and I'm not scared of plot; I don't think that's a dirty word. I enjoy the propulsive quality of other books. I think we're interested in other people, both as writers and readers. Which is not to say that I don't think the issues of the world are not important, but I think the way of making them interesting is through characters. Otherwise, your characters become cyphers, and however much people feel that they ought to be reading for their own good about these so-called issues, they won't really engage. That makes it sound like my cunning plan! But actually, these things emerge quite naturally. It would take some effort to keep them out.

SS: For *Love Marriage*, what was the germ that inspired you?

MA: I had been writing, and not writing, and putting things away for some time. I say some time, for years ... I had two different stories: Harriet, North London, liberal lovey, in one of them as the protagonist; and Yasmin, this young doctor from an Asian background in the other. But I wasn't convinced I would write either of them as a novel. Then I had the idea of putting them together, in a "light bulb" moment. I didn't know how it was going to shape out, but I had the feeling that I definitely had to write it.

That was a different genesis from previous novels, this melding between two worlds, but it made sense to me because of the duality. I'm sort of non-binary. Not in terms of gender identity, but every other aspect of my identity is non-binary. I don't feel the need to be either/or, and there isn't any remote possibility of me *not* being both. So when I've felt a sort of desire of people to put me in one place or the other, I've found it difficult. I mean, it's literally an existential issue. At times I felt that I should be able to prove that I really am both/and rather than either/or, but somehow, I was failing in some way. I think it's taken me a long time to realize, why should I?

Coming back to the process of writing the novel, *Love Marriage* was different from the previous books, where I had a very tight first draft, which hadn't been too far off from the final novel. I always edited a lot as I went along and had a road map. For this, I sort of knew what the ending was going to be, but I just wrote and wrote. I ended up with 240,000 words. I think part of that was not wanting to finish it, perhaps because of a sort of anxiety about not wanting to go through the publication process again, so I just kept writing. At the time, I thought this was not how you were supposed to do it. But then, I enjoyed the process of cutting something out of this wall of words that I had created. I thought I'd be daunted by it, that it would reveal that there was no strong underlying structural story, but it didn't turn out to be the case – it *was* there; I just had to carve it out. It was an interesting experience for me as a writer. The possibility that each book has its own way of coming into being.

I've always enjoyed the craft of putting a book together. You immerse yourself in the characters. You have to let them go where they will, but then I've always also really enjoyed working out, like a jigsaw puzzle, where everything goes, and fitting it together. That's a work of skill. I'd always seen those two elements working hand in hand, whereas, with this book, I let go of the control when I was writing. Having got to the end of editing, I thought, it doesn't mean it's the wrong process. Maybe, it's the right process for this book.

SS: You explore the power of sexuality, which I feel is the driver at so many levels in *Love Marriage.*

MA: I thought it was important to write it, and not gloss over, because that is a part of our identity; how we fall in line with other people's expectations, how we hide our own desires even from ourselves, how we limit ourselves because of societal expectations which we've imbibed and internalized, or because of the way that male/female power dynamics function. For Yasmin, it's an integral part of her growth, of her finding herself, the good bits and the bad bits of herself, and accepting them. The sex wasn't tagged on just because the story is about love marriage. It is significant also in terms of her breaking boundaries with her religion. It is much more weighted than for a character who has always been sexually free. That's why I tackled those tricky sex scenes. I've been telling anyone who asks what the book's about, that it's about love and marriage. While that's true, the engine of this novel is sex – infidelity, revenge sex, sexual addiction, covert incest, sexual violence, issues of sexual preference or identity. In narrative terms, sex is the propeller that moves the story along. In terms of character, sex is at the heart of how the protagonists struggle with their identities or mature into them. In terms of relationships and family dynamics, sex is pivotal in the creation of tension, drama, lies, and shame. In a Freudian sense, it is every character's weakness and strength.

SS: I think you managed to get a good balance of different perspectives.

MA: It's interesting what you say about the balance, which relates to where we started off, talking about writing from character. For me to write about Harriet and Joe from a distance wouldn't work – it has to grow out of having empathy with them. There's always the other side of experience. It might seem all very enviable to be in Joe's position. He's got everything handed to him: white male, privileged, rich, doctor, handsome, etcetera. But you just don't know. Again, it's this temptation to make assumptions, though more often than not, they turn out to be partially false or significantly false because each of us is complicated. You don't know who somebody is unless you've taken the time to get to know them.

SS: What were you interested in in your interrogation of class in *Love Marriage*?

MA: You can't write about British society without getting yourself entangled in class. How do those class differences play out when you intermingle them with cultural differences and from the perspective of an immigrant family? I was interested in where you lie in the social spectrum if you are educated, and a doctor, but you also have brown skin.

How does that differ from generation to generation? Is Shaokat a lot more insecure in his status than Yasmin because she was born in this country? Does Yasmin actually suffer more because she's more aware of distinctions in taste and manners and attitudes that her father might be oblivious to? Where are the agonies? That's where it becomes interesting – finding the pain points and probing at them.

SS: Class is often looked at in extremes in popular culture today.

MA: Yes, the extremes in the broader sense, so it's Boris Johnson and the toffs in Cabinet, or those from "Benefits Street", the underclass. There are so many more gradations. You could say of Yasmin's family and Joe's family, they're all just middle class. But it's much more subtle than that. It's evolving because as we change as a society, the way that class operates also changes; but one thing it does not do is disappear.

SS: Who are the characters you consider most important in *Love Marriage*?

MA: Yasmin is definitely the protagonist. The seed of the story came from Harriet and Yasmin, but once Joe was in play, I was equally interested in Joe and Harriet. Sexuality is also explored through Joe. To me, that was in keeping with other parts of the exploration of sexual preference, expression, etcetera, because sex is actually about something much bigger than sex itself. That's as true of Joe as it is of Yasmin.

SS: Harriet brought Joe up in a way that was not "repressive" and with "modern" ideas, yet it had a different effect than expected.

MA: Things which are not freedoms, which are things that bind us, sometimes present themselves as freedoms, and vice versa. Rania's headscarf is a symbol of oppression for some people, but for her, it symbolizes her freedom and her right to choose what she wears. Again, things are not as they appear.

SS: The assumption about South Asian culture is that it's not "open" and therefore "backward" ...

MA: Right. Exactly so! Yasmin kind of wavers at first, feeling a bit of admiration for how open Harriet and Joe are with each other. There's no shame, no hiding, no need for cover stories. Sexuality is celebrated rather than hidden. Early on in the book she thinks, I'm going to tell Joe this terrible story about my mum embarrassing us at dinner, that's what's wrong with our family, we're not open about things. At some point, she feels that it's not always easy to have everything out on the table when everyone's finding out everything. More fundamentally though, Harry and Joe aren't completely open, so that's a facade there, as much as there are facades within the supposedly "closed" cultures. I keep coming back to that. I enjoy diving into complexity and I think that's what the novel can do. That's what is difficult to do in other literary and artistic forms, to the same depth and same extent.

SS: We talked earlier in this interview about your interest in power relations; how does this play out in *Love Marriage*?

MA: There are three things that ignite people's interest, that are always at the heart of any really compelling story. They are money, sex, and power, aren't they?

With power, people often think that's something you experience at a societal, governmental, or political level. But actually, the story doesn't have to be on that scale. If you have two people in a room or in a relationship, who's got the power? – that's the core of every single relationship. That doesn't mean that it's static. It can shift around immensely. I've always found that interesting to explore, and how power in a relationship is perceived by the people within it or those outside it. In the relationship between Anisah and Harriet, where does the power balance lie and who is perceiving it, in what way? Yasmin has her own perspective on it, that Harriet is treating Ma like a kind of poodle, like her pet. Rania hasn't actually witnessed it, but has opinions about exotification. To her mind, it could come uncomfortably close to being racist. Harriet is exoticizing Ma, but what is the truth of that relationship? Who is actually in charge, who benefits, and who gives and receives in the relationship? It's different from what people perceive. Even within the relationship between Ma and Baba – is she the downtrodden woman? Does she have any volition? Has he mistreated her? Life is never simple, relationships aren't simple, and people aren't simple. I really like digging into those questions, to know what's underneath the surface. In *In the Kitchen*, I was exploring that more on a societal level; the strata of the guests at the hotel, the owners, the management, the different layers within the kitchen, right down to the porters and Lena. That functioned as a microcosm for me. Also, the north–south divide, the different attitudes that Gabe and his father hold, etcetera. How can one turn away from exploring issues of power in a novel?

SS: Talking about assumptions, Yasmin's mother really isn't the person Yasmin thought her to be.

MA: Exactly, we don't always think of our parents as people. Yasmin underestimates her mother, which is not to say that Yasmin is at fault necessarily. Anisah has her own role to play in that. What has she shared, and what has she not shared? Why has the relationship been constructed in that way? While it's part of Yasmin's journey to self-understanding, I don't intend it to be like, what a terrible daughter she is!

SS: Going back to the time before *Brick Lane*, why did you make a conscious effort to find out about and connect with Bangladesh?

MA: Having children had something to do with starting writing, which was a desire I'd been suppressing for some time. It also had to do with wanting to find out more about Bangladesh. My children are British, and it's not that I'm going to make them into something that they're not. Nevertheless, there's something you want to keep, acknowledge, explore, and discuss with your children. It was partly my own curiosity, but definitely having the kids sparked my desire not to lose some of those inter-generational threads. I started researching, and it *was* research – it was a deliberate seeking out, delving into, interviewing people, reading; it wasn't like it was all in me. I think that is the thing with debuts; people automatically think that's your life story. It wasn't my life story; it was something that I researched. Naila Kabeer's[1] (2000) book, *The Power to Choose: Bangladeshi Women and Labour Market Decisions in London and Dhaka*, really struck a chord with me; there's an awful lot of influence that the book has on *Brick Lane*. Naila was very generous in discussing various aspects of the book with me. I spent time on the housing estates around the Brick Lane area in East London. I went to women's centres. A majority of Bangladeshis in Britain are from Sylhet, so I couldn't write about Bangladeshis in the UK in any meaningful way without engaging with people from that background.

SS: You mentioned that you had been suppressing your desire to write for some time, so how did you get started?

MA: The immediate catalyst was my grandfather's death. We went to his funeral and since we had a booking for a holiday in the Lake District, we went straight there with the kids. There is something about a funeral that's quite galvanizing. You realize that if you don't do the things you really want to do with your life, then, at some point, it's over and you never took your chance. Simon was very understanding, so he took the children off every morning for two or three hours and I started with what eventually became *Brick Lane*. I just thought, I've got to try to do it. It was slightly mad in retrospect, wanting to be a writer. It seemed like a ludicrous idea. Allowing myself to think of it as a serious possibility helped make it feasible. I think the first time I had thought why not me, was when I read Hanif Kureishi's (1990) *Buddha of Suburbia* in my twenties. But then, you carry on with your life. I had to earn my living and I wasn't going to earn it by writing novels. That did still seem out of reach, although I always knew I wanted to write. Literature and books meant so much to me. I just never admitted it to myself that I wanted to write too.

SS: There are also other things at play; the feeling of responsibility or having a platform on which to speak up about issues of race, as a person of colour or someone with a Bangladeshi heritage, but also to be yourself, without having to speak for or represent all people of colour.

MA: Yes, it's not just in the field of arts. Rushanara Ali, a British MP of Bangladeshi origin, told me that she often gets asked about anything that has to do with Bangladeshis in the UK, although she's not the MP for all things Bangladeshi. She's the MP for all her diverse constituents. It's a double-edged thing. It's not that one never wants to do something, speak up, or engage with those issues. The questions posed to her could be well-intentioned but also deeply ignorant in the way they are framed, and that can be really galling. It's very difficult to expose it without being seen as "chippy", you know you've got a chip on your shoulder, and that's the situation Yasmin finds herself in.

In addition to that, I've always been a bit reticent about the idea of being a beacon to Bangladeshi girls, a role model. I used to think I'm definitely not a role model. I sort of shrank from it, the whole notion of it seemed to me to be dubious. Now I think I was wrong with those feelings. Because I felt the lack of it so sharply in my own childhood. It goes back to what you said about being from Bangladesh was not so cool. That's something that comes up in *Brick Lane* too. I've had a reminder about it, through my daughter in particular. She's going to see Joy Crookes on Saturday, who you may know as a singer, a pop star, but also a half Bangladeshi. And for my daughter, that's really cool, that she's half Bangladeshi too. To me, that is really meaningful because it's still largely the case that it's not cool to be Bangladeshi. That's something that's real for kids. I think I was wrong to think I can't possibly add anything meaningful to these kids' lives. Now that *Brick Lane* is an A-level text, I do talks with sixth-form kids. It extends to the mixed-race heritage of Indian British too. Those girls are so keen to talk about what it means to them. I'm so over this idea that it's not significant – it *is* significant. I embrace it now, but that's different from the idea of being asked constantly about race.

SS: It's interesting that even now, young women of mixed origin or of colour feel that it is so relevant to have role models or to look at things in a different way or through a typical lens.

MA: If you don't see yourself reflected in the culture in some way, that is a problem. It's damaging. It makes me think of the children's stories and myths and fables where it's the monsters who don't have a reflection in the mirror; you think there's something wrong with you if you don't see yourself in the culture. My writing about different things will also make it easier for people in the future. Even if it hasn't worked out perfectly, it still lays a path.

SS: You've gone in your writing where your heart or mind or intellectual curiosity has taken you?

MA: That's exactly what I was doing. Looking back, I was naive because I thought why can't I write about anything I want to write about? I didn't really understand how incomprehensible that seemed to some people. What is she running away from?

What's she hiding from? As though I was in denial about my identity. My identity embraces all of those things that I write about. My mother is English, she is white, but my father's Bangladeshi and that's where I was born. However, I've lived here almost all my life, so that plays a big part in who I am. *Brick Lane* was such a popular success; that's not a bad thing, but I think there is something else going on, which is that the brown skin is the dominant signifier. The denial is not mine. Other people are denying me my wholeness, my complete identity. It's brutally simplistic, but that's the truth of it.

SS: Right, you didn't write about what was "expected" of you after *Brick Lane*, as you did not intend to be "strategic".

MA: That would have been the way to build and retain a readership and been the smart move commercially. I knew that. But I'm not a marketing machine, I'm a writer. I'm not the only or the first writer to write across a diverse range of settings, topics, and cultures, but it is hard to do it as a brown woman. I was gaslighting myself for a long time, telling myself, "You're imagining that the reactions have anything to do with the colour of your skin, you're playing the race card to yourself." Now I stand back from it because I know what the truth is. Who cares whether people believe it or not? *I know!* This is my experience and I'm going to "own" it now.

SS: What gave you that inner conviction to stick to the trajectory of what you were writing and not get swayed by what people around you were saying, because I'm sure the pressures were enormous then?

MA: I don't know, I'm quite stubborn. I want to do what I want to do and in the way I want to do it, otherwise it's not meaningful, it'll be fake. It'll be a confection. I mean, what's the work about then?

SS: Yes, your writing is about getting to the truth.

MA: For me, the writing comes from character, and character is endlessly complicated. It's in relation to other people that our character reveals itself, and there's often a gap between our perceived "personality" and our deep character, so it's fascinating. Sometimes the process of writing is so hard, and I can't get myself in the right space, but when I'm actually in it, time goes just like that. That's the joy of it for me that I can lose myself. I used to do the same as a kid when I was reading. It really did feel like an escape to me, and I can't lose myself very often the same way now as a reader, but as a writer I can.

SS: Your exploration of how people react in different circumstances is fascinating.

MA: Right, this idea that there is a solid self somewhere ... that kind of self just doesn't exist. It's a dynamic process spatially and over time. Depending on where you are, where you happen to have been born, and in relationship to others. When I'm writing, being a parent, or doing my voluntary work, people will experience me differently. It doesn't mean that I'm dissembling; that is how people are. That is why I find it hard to do press and media stuff because, ultimately, it's fake. I like writing with freedom, complexity, depth, and layers. That's why the novel form suits me. Soundbites don't really suit me.

SS: I have read your article on feminism in *The Guardian* (Ali 2018) because I am just curious about your thoughts on it and other political and personal issues as a writer. One of the core secrets of *Love Marriage* is this horrific act of violence against women. I think we are both deeply committed to this issue, but I was wondering how you view your engagement with the feminist movement. For me, I am sometimes "out there" about it, but sometimes it is not so public.

MA: I've always considered myself a feminist. Sometimes that's the lens through which you view the world and sometimes it takes more of a back seat, but it's always there. As a mother of an adolescent, and later an older teenager and then a young woman – my daughter is 20 years old now – you can't help but think about those things. I think back and see myself at her age and see how much more aware she is and how much more she inhabits her equal rights.

That article was part of a bigger piece, where I was talking about how I was the only girl in a cohort of ten students studying politics, philosophy and economics (PPE) in my college at Oxford and felt quite grateful about it. I *cannot* imagine my daughter feeling "grateful" in a similar circumstance. She would rightly be outraged, yet I definitely considered myself a feminist and was quite vocal at the time. So, I'm always looking at the gap between perception and reality or seeking to disentangle the "theory" from what you think the world is or should be. But it's hard when you are in it.

Many young women might feel that they are feminists and empowered and may think that the way they dress or act is entirely up to them. It's very hard for them to look outside of that box because the culture is sort of hegemonic. You can't see outside of it, so I'm always thinking about those sorts of interplays. Maybe there's a connection with having a dual heritage. You're simultaneously in the box and outside the box, so it is quite a good position from which to observe. I am always intrigued by how little people can see their own reality, notwithstanding how smart they are. I think that relates a lot to the role of women as well – what we are being told or persuaded of, or what we are convincing ourselves of or what we can see and not see, etcetera.

Then you also mentioned the horrific act of violence against a woman. In recent years, there's been more visibility of acts of violence against Indian women, like the case of that young woman, Jyoti Singh, gang raped on a moving bus in New Delhi who eventually died of her injuries.[2] I went on a march the weekend that the BBC's documentary film about her, *India's Daughter* (Udwin 2015), came out.[3] I watched that film with my daughter, which was a pretty hard watch but also a necessary watch. Then we went on the International Women's Day March the next day. It was a beautiful day, with a sense of solidarity and potential. Sarah Gavron, who directed the film *Brick Lane*, gave a speech, as she was directing a film about the early feminists. You have to do both. You have to be aware of the terrible truths and also be optimistic and positive. I mean, what is marching? You're going for a walk, but you're with like-minded people and you have to believe that you can make a difference.

SS: *Love Marriage* is going to be serialized, hopefully. How is that going?

MA: I'm writing the screenplay and the TV rights are sold. That's only the start. It could be many years of trying and failing, or it could all go brilliantly well and get greenlit. The BBC commissioned the development work on the first couple of episodes. I'm enjoying translating those characters into a screenplay. That's where my focus is at the moment. That's what I would love to make happen. I've been trying for a number of years to get a screenplay commissioned and on the air, so if it did happen for *Love Marriage* that would be the culmination of a lot of hard work and learning of the craft. I think we haven't seen anything like it on TV here. There is still a bit of a lag with these multicultural stories, especially when it comes to TV.

I'm loving the screenwriting. It's so collaborative. I don't know if I would enjoy a writers' room – the American model sounds quite alien to me – but I do love the back and forth, the script meetings, tossing ideas around with other creative people and then being allowed to come back to my desk. There's a lot that's very close to the book, but I'm still creating and that process is really gratifying. I'm hoping that when the book is out, talking about it will feel more natural because my head will still be in those characters, still inventing new things about them. I'm hoping that that will help me feel more engaged in the publicity.

I'm working on the second episode on a scene that is not in the book. I'm back with Joe and Yasmin and they're in bed, and it's sort of an intimate scene that goes a little askew, shall we say. It's really forcing me to think again about their deepest motivations and fears and which of those they actually understand, and which of those they have not even recognized and don't even know themselves. I feel quite close to them again. Of course, they don't leave you altogether once you finish the book, but you stop obsessing about them. Now I'm back in that headspace. That's where I'm happiest really.

SS: With your characters?

MA: Well, anything to do with writing. The craft of it [writing for the screen] is different from the novel; you're much more constrained. You have to hit certain beats. You have to have the story hook at the end of an episode. There are certain plates you have to keep spinning because you know you're laying this in order to pick it up in episode 3. But at its root, it's about seeing and hearing the characters, and that's what I do when I'm writing prose.

When I'm teaching, I've often found that students will come with a piece of work and I'll say, in this scene on the railway platform which end of the platform are they? Most often the student doesn't know. It's not working because the writer has not actually "seen" it. If they can't envisage it, if they haven't done that creative imaginative work – and it is work – of really knowing where everything is, there is no hope of conveying it to the reader. So, scene writing for television is not that different from writing a scene for the novel. But in the technicalities, it is.

SS: Is this a medium that you want to explore more of?

MA: Definitely! I've got another TV project on the boil, which is an original idea. Strangely enough, when I didn't think I'd ever write another novel, trying my hand at screenwriting helped me get back some of that joy of writing; so although nothing came to fruition, it freed me up in a way and gave me some of that energy and desire to write again.

SS: What happened? Was it getting involved with raising your family, or was it something else? You just felt burnt out?

MA: Yes, that would be one way of putting it. The reception of *Brick Lane* was obviously largely positive, but I didn't enjoy the process that much. I felt ill a lot of the time and I didn't acknowledge that. I was constantly taking antibiotics for some infection or other; my kids were still very young, I was doing a lot of travelling, not wanting to really but feeling like I had to. Of course, there were parts I enjoyed, but overall it was hard. Then I felt a bit beaten up after three subsequent books were largely treated with a mixture of scorn and bemusement. I thought, I just don't want to do it anymore. It's not worth it. I felt depressed, I guess. That's why it's been ten years, because I just thought that I'm not going through that whole process again.

SS: I'm so glad that you've been able to get beyond that. Reading the book and talking to you, I can see that you're very much in your element.

MA: Me too, I'm glad. Trying screenwriting has made me realize that there's nothing I want to do other than write. I'm sort of alive when I'm writing.

SS: Isn't that a wonderful realization!

MA: Hahahah! Well, it could also be awful. I've got to continue doing this thing that causes me pain and anguish.

SS: I'm also excited that you have linked up with Virago.

MA: Yes, I'm so happy to be with Virago, it's such a venerable institution. The Virago Modern Classics are so brilliant and I love the way they revive some titles. Most recently, I read Attia Hosain's ([1961] 2021) *Sunlight on a Broken Column*, just brilliant ...

SS: Yes, it's a brilliant book. I think it was one of the first books I ever read by somebody from this part of the world. I must read it again.

MA: I'm sure it would stand up to a second reading. I just thought – how has this gone out of print and circulation? She's so sharp, and she has so much to say.

SS: And that's why you just need to keep writing.

MA: It's a strange little world, isn't it? This fiction reviewing and the literary circle. I mean, painters don't get that – painters reviewing other painters.

SS: Yes, and biases are in it, so reviews don't necessarily represent what readers may think.

MA: I was talking to a friend who paints, and I was saying I'm not looking forward to the reviews of *Love Marriage*, going back to it, because in some ways it's a position of vulnerability. And given the past experience, even though you try and avoid the reviews, you get to know about them because people tell you. And my painter friend replied, quite rightly, what do you have to worry about, you've got a name and a sort of "position", and that is all true. Her basic premise was, you shouldn't care about what anyone says, which is also true. Later, she showed me some negative feedback on a commission that she'd got, where she had received some comments which were quite mild, but not glowing, and she said she had been so furious and upset she couldn't sleep for a week. And I said, I totally get that, it's really awful. It hurts like hell. Well, just imagine if that was in a national newspaper, but not those mild criticisms, "insipid mush" was one phrase I got, and you know that your contemporaries are likely, or some of them are likely, to see that. Wouldn't that hurt a little bit more?

SS: Exactly! It's easy to say it, but it's a different matter when it happens to you. Even so, I'm so happy that you wrote the novel. When is the book being officially launched?

MA: The book launch is on February 3, 2022. I think I'm going to have a party for the book launch. Whatever happens – good, bad, or indifferent – I think I should celebrate.

Notes

1. Naila Kabeer is a British Bangladeshi social economist, research fellow, writer, and professor at the London School of Economics.
2. For further details on the incident, see the following Wikipedia entry: https://en.wikipedia.org/wiki/2012_Delhi_gang_rape_and_murder.
3. In addition to the BBC documentary (Udwin 2015), Canadian film-maker Richie Mehta (2019) made a seven-part television series, *Delhi Crime*. It won an Emmy Award in Best Drama Series category in 2020.

Disclosure statement

No potential conflict of interest was reported by the author.

References

Ali, Monica. 2003. *Brick Lane*. London: Doubleday.
Ali, Monica. 2006. *Alentejo Blue*. London: Doubleday.
Ali, Monica. 2009. *In the Kitchen*. London: Doubleday.
Ali, Monica. 2011. *Untold Story*. London: Simon and Schuster.
Ali, Monica 2018. "Monica Ali on Feminism in the 2000s: 'I Hadn't Truly Considered the Impact of Children'." *The Guardian*. https://www.theguardian.com/lifeandstyle/2018/feb/01/2000s-feminism-monica-ali-third-wave-plurality
Ali, Monica. 2022. *Love Marriage: A Novel*. London and New York: Vintage.
Hosain, Attia. [1961] 2021. *Sunlight on a Broken Column*. London: Virago.

Kabeer, Naila. 2000. *The Power to Choose: Bangladeshi Women and Labor Market Decisions in London and Dhaka.* London and New York: Verso.

Kureishi, Hanif. 1990. *Buddha of Suburbia.* London: Faber.

Mehta, Richie. dir. 2019. *Delhi Crime. TV Series.* Mumbai and Los Angeles, CA: Golden Caravan and Ivanhoe Pictures.

Powers, Richard. 2021. *Bewilderment.* London: Heinemann.

Udwin, Leslee. dir. 2015. *India's Daughter.* London: British Broadcasting Corporation (BBC) Storyville Series.

Index

For Product Safety Concerns and Information please contact our EU representative GPSR@taylorandfrancis.com
Taylor & Francis Verlag GmbH, Kaufingerstraße 24, 80331 München, Germany

www.ingramcontent.com/pod-product-compliance
Lightning Source LLC
Chambersburg PA
CBHW081358090726
47908CB00011B/2717

* 9 7 8 1 0 3 2 6 7 0 3 6 2 *